LIVING IN AMSTERDAM

Brigitte Forgeur
Photographs by Christian Sarramon

Cees Nooteboom
Max van Rooy
Arend Jan van der Horst

Thames and Hudson

Translated from the French
L'Art de Vivre à Amsterdam
by Jacqueline Taylor

The photograph on p.173 is by Rollan Didier,
all the others by Christian Sarramon

First Published in Great Britain in 1992
Reprinted 1997

CONTENTS

WATER,
WATER EVERYWHERE

In the course of the centuries,
the street-plan of Amsterdam has grown
into a well-ordered maze of canals,
a magic semicircle which has stamped its
mark on the world. Nothing has changed
in this city planned and fashioned by men
and by water. The city is an open book
and the walker its reader.

By Cees Nooteboom

First of all, the land. The North Sea beats against a range of dunes, meets resistance and rolls on, grey-green, grey-brown, until it finds a way through. Then it edges round the land, forcing through the weak spots to the other side where it spreads out into the Waddenzee – the Dutch shallows – and then the Zuiderzee – the southern sea. Then with its strong arm, the IJ (pronounced 'eye'), it scoops out the same stretch of land from behind. Between one sea and the other is a waste of land-spits and salt flats at the mercy of the all-powerful water, protected only by puny dykes of bladderwrack holding together the vegetation of weeds and rushes which the local people burn to make the soil workable. A place sparsely populated with farmers and fishermen – water people caught between the streams, the mudflats and the waterways, living on reclaimed land beside the rivers, always threatened by the rising water-level, the settling peat-bogs, by storms and tidal waves.

In this way not only a land but a race of people has come into being, a people that has not discovered its land, nor been given it, but has created it. Stacking the turves of peat into a wall across the fields, the farmers fight against the sea's sucking and tugging, its perpetual assault. Everywhere on the low land the inhabitants raise dykes to contain the rising water to the east, building themselves houses of loam, reeds and timber. Once the locks are in place they can drain away the water, all its power spent, back into the sea which returns again and again to the attack. If they are to survive they cannot afford to let nature take its course, and every little community organizes itself for a united struggle against invasion by the watery enemy. The land is marshy and vulnerable under a wide, changing sky with a flat horizon broken only by the western dunes – the Dutch mountains – which have

In the aptly named Low Countries, pools of water were left where the peat-bogs had been cut – pale mirrors reflecting the flight of birds and with thatched farmhouses perched on their banks (preceding pages).

Beneath the infinity of the sky lies the monumental horizontality of the Zuiderzee (the southern sea), held back by man-made dykes. When you follow the straight, tussocky roads that run below sea level, you are reminded of the proud national saying that, if God created the earth, the Dutch made Holland (opposite).

The flight of countless seagulls constantly catching the eye reminds us that, as well as being in a land that welcomes free spirits, we are in a haven for birds of all kinds. They are everywhere, at once familiar and exotic: terns, herring-gulls, grey herons, as well as ducks such as the mallard (above).

one sea in front of them and another behind: Noordzee, the northern sea, and Zuiderzee, the southern sea. A river meanders across the land of Amestelle. The Counts of Holland and the Bishops of Utrecht both lay claim to this wet, shapeless marshland in a forsaken corner of Lower Lorraine. *Stelle*: a safe, sheltered place; *Ame*: water. The land gives its name to the winding river. The river loops round the higher ground then curves across land that begs for straight lines with the languid sinuousness of a baroque volute. Where it flows into the Zuiderzee the long inlet is called the IJ, and on the banks of the IJ the river conjures up a city, a city on the waterside. Now the scene is set.

The river stamps its mark like a signet on the shore, defining its form like a skilful calligrapher. Once seen, never forgotten – over the centuries the map of Amsterdam has become an increasingly complex sign, a Chinese character developing endless ramifications yet never changing its meaning. The land is the paper, the water the ink. Like an oriental master, the river has drawn the first stroke with effortless precision, a stroke of the utmost simplicity. The people take up the brush and become a collective calligrapher. They have all the time in the world. So far they have taken eight hundred years and the character they have created is a well-ordered labyrinth of concentric canals intersecting with a network of waterways and defensive works, an enclosed cosmos, a magic semicircle that has impressed its mark on the world. The river and the ocean estuary that it flows into, linking it to the rest of the world, still form its main axis. Between and along these waterways the city has branched out into its present shape. Each new line in the drawing is a moment of its history – economic, political, cadastral. Each stroke of the calligrapher's brush has been dictated by wars, power-

struggles, economic fluctuations, discoveries, profits, defence requirements, consolidation. The concentric series of seaward canals grows into one of Europe's mightiest strongholds and the ships that leave the city, to return only after many years, sail to the ends of the earth and carry its name and fame to the far tropics and the frozen wastes of the northern seas, adding their own strokes to the ever-growing character.

Dreaming plains, grassy and green, criss-crossed by modest canals which cut across the pasture-lands, weaving their threads of grey-blue or silver according to time or weather beneath the ever-changing sky (right).

In the picturesque Zaan region, a river whose sleepy banks are bordered by fishing villages with typical wooden houses. Once, great merchant ships of the biggest fleet in the world sailed these waters. In this region Peter the Great, incognito, worked as an apprentice shipwright (left).

The Zuiderzee, formed through the course of centuries out of the delta created by numberless streams and rivers, was the cradle of Amsterdam. From its banks, painters observed and drew the sailing-ships which were one of the favourite subjects of classical Dutch painting. Since the *Afsluitdijk* (enclosing dyke), that eighteen-mile masterpiece of Dutch engineering genius, was completed in 1932, this sea has been transformed into a huge inland lake, the IJsselmeer. Muiden, a little fishing village and boating harbour at the mouth of the Vecht, has been reflected in these waters for nearly eight centuries (following pages).

Water in all its aspects: as ice, as snow, as reflecting surface, as vapour. . . . In winter, the whole landscape seems to turn to mineral and confers on everything a purity that is softly veiled by the northern mists. Tradition perpetuates age-old rites and, just as in old pictures, Avercamp's for example, you can see skaters gliding across the frozen lakes and canals. And against the background of the ocean sky the slender form of a heron sometimes comes to rest like a hieroglyph on some forgotten landing-stage.

What, after all, is a city made of? Everything that has ever been said, dreamed, destroyed, created there. All that has been built up and knocked down, every unrealized vision. The living and the dead. The wooden houses later demolished or burnt down, the bridge over the IJ that was designed but never built. The old houses still standing, full of the memories of past generations. But there is much more than that. A city is the sum of all the words that were ever spoken within its walls, an endless murmuring, whispering, singing and shouting, heard once then gone with the wind. Yet not quite gone, for these words were once part of the city and, even though lost for ever, made their mark simply by being there, by being shouted or spoken here at some moment of a winter's night or a summer's day. The sermon preached in the open air, the verdict of a court, the cry of a man being flogged, the bidding at an auction, proclamations, edicts, demonstrations, pamphlets, the announcement of a death, the watchman calling the hours, the words of nuns and whores, kings and regents, painters, aldermen, hangmen, sea-captains, soldiers, lock-keepers and builders – a continuous dialogue along the canals in the living heart of the city, this in itself is the city. Anyone can hear if he cares to listen. It lives on in archives, poetry, street names and proverbs, in the words and inflections of the language, just as the faces in paintings by Frans Hals and Rembrandt are still there to be seen today, and as our own words and faces will one day vanish among those other words and faces, remembered and unremembered, carried off, forgotten yet still present, contained in the word that is also the city: Amsterdam.

A seventeenth-century sailor dying of scurvy on the island of Amboina saw a vision of the city, his city that he was never to see again. What he

NOACHS ARCK

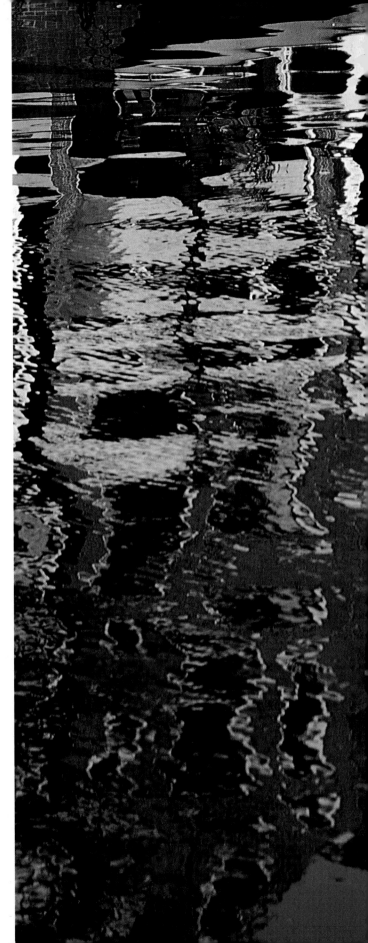

The city is a reflection, at once firm and intangible, in which the eye is caught at every turn by some symbol loaded with history, such as the sculpted stones on the gables of the houses that are mirrored in the impressionistic ripples of the canals. Who knows if this surface, broken up for a trembling moment, may not have inspired Van Gogh's whirlwind of brushstrokes from which the image emerged transformed?

In the seventeenth century, the Golden Age, the time of Rembrandt, Amsterdam overflowed with wealth amassed from the four corners of the world. These traders could hardly be said to have baroque souls, and yet . . . this patrician house on the Keizersgracht, the Emperor's Canal, is surely one of the exceptions that prove the rule (left).

Very close to the broad 17th-century canals built at the height of the city's greatness, a linking network of small transverse canals was created, given the names of flowers and trees and inhabited until recently by artisans and sailors. The district is called the Jordaan, a name derived from the French *jardin*, garden. One of the Jordaan's canals (right) is the Bloemgracht (Flower Canal).

saw at that moment is still there in the way I see the Schreierstoren, the Weepers' Tower, where sailors used to take leave of their wives. The city is a book for the reading, the pedestrian is the reader. He can start at any page, walking backwards or forwards in time and space. The book may have a beginning but it is still a long way from its end. Its words are tablets set in walls, the holes in the ground where new buildings will rise, names, dates, statues. One house called De Pelikaan (The Pelican) has much to say of distant travels. Another called Spitsbergen evokes winters spent in icy northern seas. A street is called Bokkinghangen – Bloater-hanging – and without smelling a thing you can recall the aroma of smoked herrings. A wall plaque over a modern

Familiar visions of that magic world that is Amsterdam: watery avenues opening up like so many pages of memory; pot-bellied barges in the shade of the elms; passers-by who always seem to have a meditative air, carried away perhaps, like Rembrandt on his walks, by a train of thought evoked by this water that brings a breath of the ocean right in to the muffled hubbub of the city centre. If you know where to look, you will see that the 'Venice of the North' really exists.

doorway shows a golden gate; the walker's inner eye re-creates the golden gateway that once stood on the spot. The city is not silent, it utters words. Melkmeisjesbruggetje – the Milkmaids' Little Bridge; Varkenssluis – Pig Lock; Kalverstraat – Calf Street. The walker's imagination responds to the names dropped by history and sees a cattle-market in the street, with pens for calves here, oxen there, sheep further down. Gebed zonder End – Prayer-without-End: a narrow alley mockingly named by some citizen of earlier times who thought there were too many convents in the city centre; here prayer ceaselessly followed prayer and the name raises echoes of Gregorian chant and the high, thin female voices of the nunneries. Vijgendam – Fig Dyke: because a cargo of figs rejected by the Syndics served to plug a gap in the canal wall at this spot. The walker pauses where excavations for a new building have begun; he watches archaeologists sifting the earth, studying it minutely, scratching it with a cautious finger-nail as they rediscover the past, searching for evidence of their forefathers. He is amazed that they were able to live so far below the surface.

Like giant clasps, innumerable bridges stretch the curve of their arch over the corset of canals that grips the city. Alike yet never identical, they have an unstressed charm that is enhanced by repetition.

Does the earth grow fatter with age? He wonders if he would be able to understand the speech of those earlier Amsterdammers. Some time later he is in the museum contemplating the objects discovered in this way: shoes immediately identifiable as such – he could wear them with no trouble. Footwear, bowls, hammers, coins. But the past is not only underfoot, it is above our heads as well in the gabled roofs with their carvings of whalebones, Indians, their emblems, exotic merchandise, slaves, ships. Everyone, it seems, had something to do with ships in those days, everyone belonged to the water, the same water that still flows dark and mysterious through the canals and was so much wilder and greyer outside the city – the ocean water that brought ships sailing close in to shore, 'a forest of a thousand masts'. An old map drawn in 1544 by Cornelis Anthonisz. shows the city with its ships. There are as yet few canals dividing the area within the city walls. The city's heyday, the Golden Age, is still to come, but the IJ is already a forest of masts. Where the central railway station will one day stand, smaller boats can sail right into the city, but the heavier vessels – and there are dozens of them – have to stay out in the roads. The two great churches, hemmed in by a closely packed mass of houses on either side of the harbour, still stand as they did then. The broad waters of the Damrak extended to the site of the present Royal Palace, dividing the little town into two halves, the 'Old Side' and the 'New Side'. Our sharp-eyed walker recognizes some of the buildings, and the street plan. That city is still here for him; he walks there every day, but in the place where his house will be built in the seventeenth century there is still a red mill and there is green countryside around the city, a city that will leap to the far bank of each new canal, spreading wider on each succeeding map. Ever

In Amsterdam every paving-stone has a story to tell. But the past is not only at our feet, it is also above our heads on the gables of the houses with stones bearing symbols of the various crafts. Like the sign with two armchairs which sums up two centuries of craftsmanship in the Jordaan: a traditional rustic seat and an elegant French chair fashioned by an exiled Huguenot, accompanied by the motto 'Never Perfect' (below).

At the end of the 18th century, the port of Amsterdam harboured more than 2,500 merchant vessels which supplied the whole of Europe, in many cases with exotic products from all over the globe. Nowadays, closing your eyes in the midst of the quays and landing-stages such as this one with its sculptured figures on the Oosterdok (East Dock), you can almost hear the wind in the rigging and the hurly-burly of the cargoes being unloaded (right).

wider, because fame and prosperity grow with the growing fleets of the Companies. First the Herengracht – the Gentlemen's Canal, asserting the power of the merchant class. Only after them come the Keizersgracht and Prinsengracht – the Emperor's and Princes' Canals. Between the other, crosswise, canals bearing the names of trees and flowers – Lily, Eglantine, Rose, Laurel – the ordinary people lived in a district called the Jordaan: shipwrights, dockers, sailors, men with loud voices who brought the air of the wide world into these narrow streets.

Today is grey and misty. Closing his eyes, the walker can hear the wind in the rigging of all those cogs, caravels, frigates, galleons, brigantines, brigs; he can smell the spices, hear the many languages of the great throng of foreigners who have found refuge in his city – Portuguese and Spanish Jews, Huguenots, Flemish Calvinists, and also individuals like Descartes who found the noise of barrels rolled across the quayside conducive to meditation, or Diderot, surprised at '*cette liberté, compagne de l'indépendance, qui ne s'incline que devant les lois*' (this freedom which goes hand in hand with independence and bows its head to none but the law). There is no end to this walk, and in his mind's eye the walker reads the images one by one as they present themselves: Avercamp's skaters on the frozen canals, the medieval processions celebrating the Miracle of Amsterdam, the palatial new residences of the slave-traders, and those same slave-traders bellowing their solemn psalms beneath the vaults of the austere churches, stripped of all their ornaments by iconoclasts, that we know from Saenredam's paintings. But there are also the clandestine churches hidden away in attics, those of the persecuted Catholics; and the hanged girl sketched by Rembrandt; the poet Bredero who

Amsterdam as we see it today is a city of the 17th and 18th centuries whose time-mellowed brick seems to have a mysterious affinity with water. Like this hospice (above) and the houses that overlook the Amstel, the vast liquid artery punctuated with locks and crossed by broad bridges that was the starting point from which the city has grown outwards. It is in such places, where the historic houses stand right on the water without an intervening quay that the similarity of Amsterdam to Venice is most striking. This direct contact between houses and water is now only to be seen in a very few places in the city (as at the left of the illustration opposite). These are the backs of houses rising directly from the water of the Damrak.

drowned himself beneath the ice; the death of Hendrickje and the dispersal of Rembrandt's treasures; the revolt of the Anabaptists and their terrible punishment; the taste for luxury and the cold greed that supplied it; the burdens of wealth; the rousing cheers of greeting for national or foreign monarchs; the swaggering gait of the occupying invader – Spanish, French, German. So he arrives at his own time – the persecution of Jews in those years when the city was mutilated for ever; the places where Resistance fighters were tortured or shot; the entry of the Canadians at the Liberation – a concentration of history, the ever-renewed layers which the city has absorbed and preserved, which survive in monuments and in small, barely visible commemorative plaques and the memories of the living; the words of humiliation and defeat as well as the triumphant shouts of victories ancient and modern; Morality, Memory.

Evening falls on the city. In the fine houses that line the canals the lights are turned on, reducing everything to the dimensions of a sitting-room. There is a gentle melancholy that hangs over ports, where the nostalgia of parting is always in the air. I, the walker, pass before the Palace on the Dam which at one time, newly built, towered over all the other buildings. It stands on more than thirteen thousand piles on the same marshy ground as ever, the land of Amestelle. Here as a boy in 1948 I saw the 'old Queen', Wilhelmina, when she abdicated after a reign of fifty years. Where now wide streets run and a late-running tram looms up, ships once moored right in the heart of the city. I know where the Stock Exchange was, and the one that replaced it, and the one after that; where the Weighhouse stood, and the Fish Market; the place where the condemned were broken on the wheel, and where grain was traded. Now I walk

along canals where walked the poets who wrote my secret language which no foreigner can read: Hooft, Vondel, Bredero, Hoornik, Slauerhoff. I pass aristocrats' palaces, now office buildings, and the trading houses of a vanished empire; I can make out on a high pediment the imposing coat-of-arms of the United East India Company; and in the dark low streets of the Jordaan I pass the houses of the nameless folk of the past without whom that vanished empire, as wide as the world itself, could never have existed. Nothing has stayed the same, yet nothing has changed. It is my city, to be read only by the initiated. It will never reveal itself entirely to the stranger who does not know its language and its history, because it is precisely language and history that preserve its secret moods, secret places, secret memories. Open city, closed city. One city for us, another for the rest. A city on the water, a city of people, created and written by its people and its water. A city of many times and a city in time. A city that exists twice over, visibly and invisibly, made of stone and wood and water and of something not to be defined in words.

Twilight, the time when the transparent rectangles of the windows light up to show their interiors, whose calm occupants move 'rarely, like chessmen' (Apollinaire). Evening silence, the last golden brilliance of the sun, a peace that seems almost rural at the heart of the silent, immobile city (right).

Who could fail to admire the elegance of the hand on the gable-stone of a *hofje* in the Jordaan (below), perhaps that of a public scribe of the 17th century? This mixture of past and present that greets the casual stroller is one of the great charms of Amsterdam.

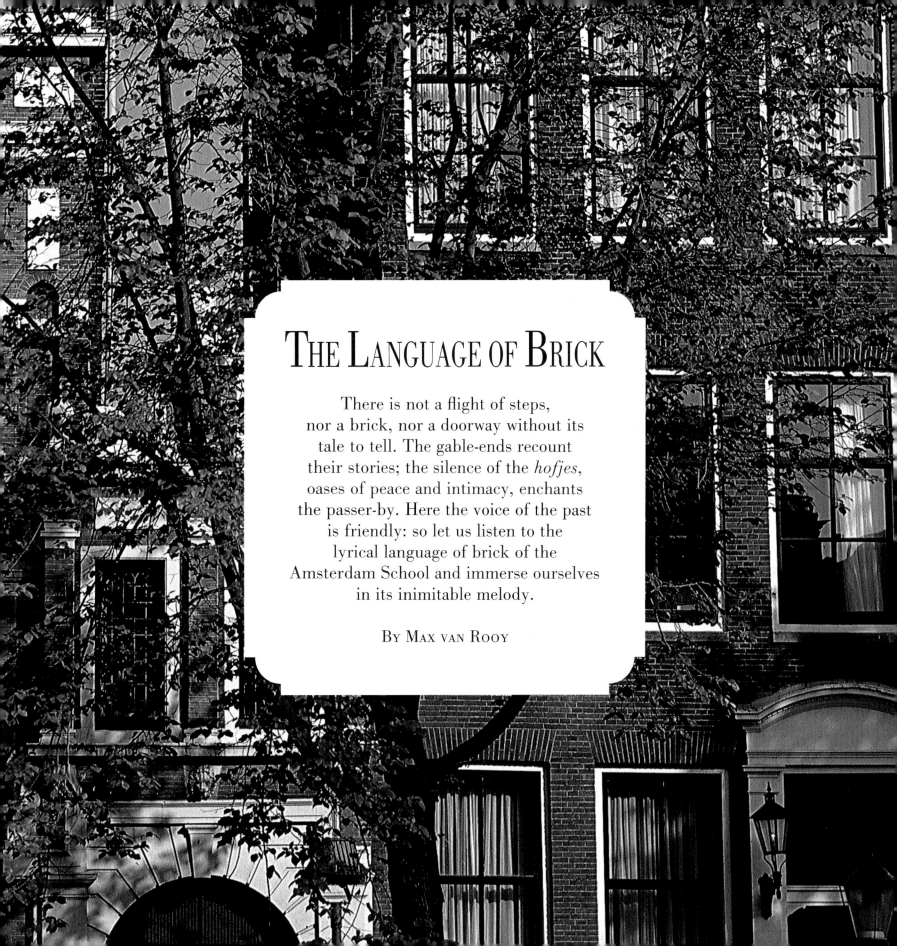

THE LANGUAGE OF BRICK

There is not a flight of steps,
nor a brick, nor a doorway without its
tale to tell. The gable-ends recount
their stories; the silence of the *hofjes*,
oases of peace and intimacy, enchants
the passer-by. Here the voice of the past
is friendly: so let us listen to the
lyrical language of brick of the
Amsterdam School and immerse ourselves
in its inimitable melody.

BY MAX VAN ROOY

There are modern architects who claim to create buildings that 'make a statement'. In Holland, a country of legendary common sense whose inhabitants have been called 'Calvin's people', such a declaration of intent will only provoke one reaction: 'Your building is no good – do you think people can live in a statement?' A statement is a drawing, a two-dimensional design, good enough perhaps for the glossy pages of a specialist magazine but quite unsuitable to create an environment, to make a pleasant setting to live in. History, on the other hand, is a place you can live in. This is how my life in Amsterdam seems to me. In this city I live both in a context of history and as a result of that history, and the consciousness of this, drawing on insatiable curiosity about the historic background of a metropolis of modest dimensions but celebrated for its culture, leaves me a perpetually astonished and therefore a happy inhabitant.

My house is in the oldest part of the heart of the city. The contours of its narrow, not very tall façade recall a simplified reproduction of Michelangelo's Porta Pia in Rome. Not that anything about it resembles the profusion of baroque ornament that adorns the Roman gateway, but the perfect symmetry of the structure, with its side pilasters surmounted by a triangular pediment – the Porta Pia of a child's tracing – is enough to evoke an image of that monument. A good old Dutch lifting-beam has replaced the inscribed plaque and the garland, and an elegant little window has taken the place of the human mask, a fanlight of refined taste such as can be seen over the doorways of most of Amsterdam's older façades. This is the famous light of the painters, of Rembrandt and Vermeer, just as famous as the cloudy Dutch skies whose ever-changing, fitful illumination continuously transforms the city.

On the Keizersgracht (preceding pages), the house on the left dates from the 17th century, while that on the right, of about the same period, was remodelled in the 19th century. The houses along the canals have been through endless modifications, so that their architecture is a way of reading the social history of the city.

A completely symmetrical façade is a rarity in these historic houses. This one (above) beside one of the canals in the Jordaan is an exception. The design of the windows with their wooden glazing bars is proof that this façade dates from the 18th century. Around 1700, in fact, the old-style mullions and transoms were replaced by sash windows.

The Amsterdam skyline is even and gentle – only Hendrick de Keyser's steeples point their fingers heavenwards. Below, the house-boats, indisputable havens of peace to the Amsterdammer's imagination (opposite).

It is half-past five in the evening and after a day of storms and fierce winds the winter sun, already sinking, shines through the clouds. Transfixed, I stop on the Halvemaanbrug, the Half-Moon Bridge, which crosses the Amstel in the direction of the Kloveniersburgwal, the Harquebusier's Rampart. The lights that line its span glimmer against the backdrop of the city and the scene before me has a breathtaking beauty. The prevailing tones are golden yellow, red, white and grey. The Hotel de l'Europe blazes in an incandescent glow. The Munttoren (Mint Tower) almost disappears, a slender silhouette against a medieval sky dappled by golden rays between the clouds. And – I swear I'm not dreaming – above Waterlooplein (Waterloo Square) there appears a flawless rainbow, clean-cut as glass, with the white marble panels of the Muziektheater (Opera House) at its geometric centre. Even at this moment of visual violence which turns the usual notions of beauty upside down, I remain convinced that the red-brick fly tower should have been coloured white. That would have been enough to charm a rainbow, I think, but architecture is arrogant and listens to nobody. This is demonstrated by its successes as well as its failures, by the Beurs van Berlage (Berlage's Stock Exchange) on the Damrak as well as by that monstrous mastodon of a building, the Nederlandse Bank, which disfigures Frederiksplein. On that spot once stood the Dutch version of London's Crystal Palace, the Paleis van Volksvlijt (Palace of National Industry), a cast-iron and glass monument ravaged by fire in 1928 which still awakens feelings of regret and nostalgia.

Now the phantasmagoric light fades. The rainbow vanishes and the monuments revert to their normal appearance and surroundings. The blaze at the Hotel de l'Europe dies down and the

building becomes its old self, a romantic, classical set-piece erected in 1895 with an acute sense of cosmopolitan decorum on the site of a rotunda where a joiner and a captain of artillery had dwelt. The spire of the picturesque Mint Tower, added to the building in 1619 by Hendrick de Keyser, the most famous of the architects who created seventeenth-century Amsterdam, at last recovers its original outline. I can even distinguish the electric wires and the multicoloured lights which will shortly, as night falls, try to create a carnival atmosphere round the little monument which seems not quite at home in this district. The exterior of the Muziektheater, still glowing a moment ago, now has a look of glum resignation. The locals have nicknamed this complex, combining Town Hall (Stadhuis) and Opera House, the 'Stopera'; one might add that this building, finally completed to the design of Cees Dam and the Viennese architect Wilhelm Holzbauer and opened in 1986, had one of the longest and most controversial gestations in the history of Amsterdam. 'You need time to get used to my being here, but it's just as difficult for me', this multiracial hybrid seems to murmur. A few

Water, canals, the trees that line them, and the *Amsterdammertjes* – the little reddish-brown cast-iron bollards which keep cars off the pavements – all these are obligatory elements for the painter who seeks to capture the peaceful atmosphere of early morning in Amsterdam (above and right).

The marble panels of the façade of the Muziektheater (Opera House) are reflected in the rippling waters of the Amstel (left). Before the last war, this island in the centre of the city was the domain of Jewish hawkers. After the war – and the deportations of so many Jews by the occupying forces – the flea-market reclaimed possession of Waterlooplein. But the Jews were not there for the reunion.

moments earlier, under the rainbow, it showed far less modesty.

Such, then, is the true aspect of the Hotel de l'Europe, the Mint Tower, the 'Stopera'. What I had glimpsed a few minutes earlier was a vision of them, a series of views of monuments taken out of context by an unusual light, briefly isolated from their urban surroundings. An exceptional moment had granted me a glimpse of the images of Amsterdam that may exist in the mind of a foreigner who has never seen the city, monuments shorn of their true proportions, with no particular location in the urban landscape, standing by pavements and streets that lack any fixed dimension.

Which of the monuments of Amsterdam most resemble their photographic images? In other words, to what extent are photographs authentic? I think it is the oldest and the newest dwellings that correspond most closely. On the one hand, then, the patrician residences of the seventeenth and eighteenth centuries which stand along the canals and, almost collapsing under the weight of history, have popularized the picturesque aspect of Amsterdam to the point of cliché all over the world; on the other, the dwellings built in the centre since the end of the sixties as part of the urban renewal programme – the houses with no history at all. There are examples of this second category in the district bounded by the Nieuwmarkt (New Market) and Rembrandt's house in the Jodenbreestraat (Broad Street of the Jews). Here, the imaged object and the image are barely distinguishable in the extent to which the rhythm of door and window openings, the articulation of façades and the decorative elements such as the little balconies are based on the simplest module of human proportions, so familiar as to leave no room for doubt. The patrician mansions beside the canals, for their part, correspond to their

The House on the Three Canals, the only house in Amsterdam that can lay claim to the name (right). It looks out on the Oudezijds Achterburgwal, the Oudezijds Voorburgwal and the Grimburgwal. Designed in 1610 by Claes Adriaans, it has housed some of Amsterdam's most glorious names down the centuries. It has an extremely fine stepped gable and the most elegant leaded windows in the city.

Many 17th-century houses look down on the passer-by from their *oeil-de-boeuf* window, its oval shape usually outlined in sandstone. This one is crowned by a neck-gable with a triangular pediment (below).

image because the main doorway, with or without steps up to it, is almost always the most important feature of the façade, and the canal banks are nearly all lined with trees. This makes two elements of scale – three if you count the height of the steps – which spare us the imaginative effort of too great a leap between image and reality.

That is of course only the second reason why the canals of Amsterdam never disappoint. The first, clearly, is the intrinsic beauty of the canals themselves and of the majestic dwellings of the Golden Age, of the history that each of them enfolds, giving them the character and depth of living beings. Wealthy beings, for the most part, some of them positively wallowing in affluence. And – let us be frank – the past history of that class of beings inspires us with a curiosity of a different order from that of a poor man's house, touching in its simplicity, in the picturesque working-class quarter of the Jordaan. It is the difference between sublimating the envy provoked by a mysterious accumulation of wealth and carrying out a sociological investigation.

The historic process of Amsterdam's commercial prosperity – a prosperity which was naturally a deciding factor in the city's physical aspect – still seems an improbable fairy-tale to me. It must be mentioned at this point for it is closely identified with the cultural history, and therefore with the form, of the city.

Towards the middle of the thirteenth century a small colony of men and women from Waterland and West Friesland settled on the banks of the IJ by the mouth of the Amstel. They managed to survive by keeping cattle and by fishing and sailing, and the watery element held no secrets for them. A dam was built across the Amstel creating a vast harbour, the Damrak. Due to the presence of this port and to the talent for

Another *oeil-de-boeuf*, which seems to spy on the passer-by and conceals a tiny room or a shadowy attic (above). Once you begin to notice these historic details, you discover an inexhaustible source of architectural poetry.

The House with the Heads at No. 123 Keizersgracht has one of the most remarkable double façades in Amsterdam. It was built in 1662, probably by the son of Hendrick de Keyser. The six heads which decorate the façade represent classical deities. Having passed through the hands of a succession of fortunate occupants, this lovely house has since 1983 been the headquarters of the Municipal Service for Historical Monuments (opposite).

navigation and trade of the Amsterdammers, those Phoenicians of the North, the modest colony beside the Amstel soon increased in population, power and wealth. At first its income derived principally from trade with the Baltic, the foundation of Amsterdam's business connections. The exploitation of another commercial resource which was to prove inexhaustible, that of the East Indies, had to wait for the beginning of the Golden Age and the foundation in 1602 of the celebrated United East India Company, followed in 1621 by the West India Company which claimed the monopoly of trade with the east coast of America and controlled the small banking operation of Nieuw Amsterdam on Manhattan Island by the mouth of the Hudson River. This modest establishment was to grow into New York, where a main thoroughfare such as Wall Street still follows the capricious route of a Dutch cow-track.

Amsterdam, for its part, became in a few decades the first western commercial metropolis. The freedom-loving city saw a rapid growth in its population, in large measure due to foreign immigrants. The Portuguese Jews expelled from Antwerp had no problems in integrating with the large merchant bourgeoisie, and Jews fleeing from Germany and Poland found work in the tobacco and diamond industries. After the Revocation of the Edict of Nantes in 1685 hundreds of Huguenots arrived from France seeking refuge in the United Provinces, among their ranks many highly skilled craftsmen who were welcomed with open arms by the city fathers of Amsterdam. Finally, in the course of the seventeenth and eighteenth centuries great numbers of German and Scandinavian emigrants arrived to settle in Amsterdam.

This cosmopolitan melting-pot in which the regents and merchants accumulated unimagin-

able wealth produced the Grachtengordel (Canal Girdle), laid out and built from 1610 onwards as the city expanded. Three canals were dug, extended on the western side by a huge area intended for the bourgeoisie and the working class and for industrial use, the Jordaan. Nowadays the Jordaan is a delightful, picturesque quarter full of little houses preserved like so many historic monuments as well as modern dwellings kept to the scale of their surroundings but nonetheless occasionally interrupting the poetic rhythm of history. If you are looking for a typical example of the legendary Dutch *gezelligheid*, that atmosphere of warm intimacy, it is here that you will find it, enriched by a profusion of architectural detail.

Among the wealthy, those who were seeking an aristocratic life-style fought hard to acquire a dwelling on one of the canals. It was a point of honour for them to embellish the decoration inside and out with features that announced their riches and their social prestige – the two generally went hand in hand. In its essence, however, the beauty of the canals is to be found less in the architecture of the façades than in the harmony of proportion between the size of the buildings, the breadth of the quays and canals, and the position and height of the trees. The canals thus create avenues of water, like no others in the world, and Tsar Peter the Great was inspired by them – notably by the trees – in planning St Petersburg. He entrusted the design of the Russian city to architects who were mostly Italian, and the resemblance is quite striking. A painting of 1685 by Gerrit Berckheyde shows the curve of the Herengracht, better known as the 'Golden Bend' because it brought together the most beautiful and the most luxurious of the patrician residences. The trees are as yet conspicuous by their absence; the bare walls are striking

The stroller in Amsterdam should constantly raise his eyes, because it is at the highest points of the gables that the most interesting and unexpected scenes take place. There, outlined against the sky, stories are told, legends are played out, characters are sketched. Simple bell-gables or stepped gables are sometimes modest and unpretentious (above). Or there are more exuberant types, like the neck-gable decorated with Negroes and Indians that crowns a merchant's house with a heavily painted façade, situated at No. 187 Oudezijds Voorburgwal (opposite).

in their austere verticality. Walking around St Petersburg (still called Leningrad at that time) I was reminded more than once of that old picture of the Herengracht.

But by far the most-quoted nickname for Amsterdam is of course 'Venice of the North'. This comparison was always inevitable, given the ubiquity of water in both cities. One of the first authors to dwell on this resemblance in her writings was the French novelist and *femme galante* Madame de Villedieu, who spent ten days in Amsterdam in 1667. After mentioning the obvious similarities – water, buildings on piles – she also reflected on the differences. In Venice there are painted and gilded gondolas manoeuvring on the canals, whereas Amsterdam's boats are manned by 'undisciplined bourgeois' who have never got into the habit of giving way to foreigners of whatever social class, while she would have us believe that in Venice one only meets refined noblemen. And she notes how Amsterdam is full of people from all over the world, whose variety of race and colour reminds her of ancient Babylon: 'No Persian, no Armenian can fail to feel as much at home here as in his own country.'

With the exception of her remark about Venetian noblemen, a good number of Madame de Villedieu's observations are still as valid today as they were three hundred years ago. This is true also of the numerous descriptions of the centre of Amsterdam which have been published over the centuries. How could it be otherwise? The main features of the ring of canals have hardly changed in their overall appearance since the Golden Age. A few canals have been filled in. Many buildings have been converted to other uses: this has happened to most of the warehouses, transformed into elegant, much sought-after flats without losing any of their characteristic outward

features, with their heavy wooden shutters. In addition, the thoughtful conservation of the patrician mansions has permitted a whole swathe of history to be kept alive, and in the last few years the will to preserve the past has visibly gathered strength. The old houses are now quite rightly treated with reverential respect. The colours of the trees, the shades of greenery along the Herengracht, are reproduced repeatedly in the paintwork of the doors and window frames.

The old city of Amsterdam contains dozens of little courtyards (*hofjes*). These miniature historic districts are still inhabited by 'senior citizens', although some of the little houses, remodelled and joined together, now offer younger generations a place to live that is as elegant as it is peaceful. The Jordaan district, in particular, conceals a great number of these little oases of intimacy and calm, often embellished with fountains (above).

The Begijnhof (right) is the most famous and the best-preserved jewel of this priceless collection. At No. 34 is one of only two remaining buildings constructed entirely of wood – vestiges of the 15th century – to be found in the city (left). The other is at No. 1 Zeedijk. The building of wooden façades was prohibited in 1669 because of the seriousness of the risk of fire.

Glancing up at the large windows, the passer-by can confirm that on the inside the original decoration has been relieved of the layers of superfluous panelling and accretions of pine wainscoting which smothered it in the fifties, sixties and seventies. The doorway of the historic house has been restored to its original contours and the term 'old-fashioned' has lost much of its pejorative force. In the last ten years the centre of Amsterdam has been freed from the blinkered, egalitarian and unimaginative modernism of the post-war years.

Just as the idea of water is inseparable from the history of a city whose name derives from a dam and a river (the Amstel), so warehouses are essential components of a city whose economic importance derives from the sea and from commercial acumen. The map of Amsterdam shows hundreds of ancient warehouses. Recognizable from their round-headed openings, heavy shutters of solid wood and huge lifting-beams, they often bear names that evoke exotic continents or mythological figures. They were built in an era of prosperity which did not last: the port of Amsterdam silted up and the warehouses were left empty. The proud structures began to decay, and it was not until well after the Second World War that it was realized that such buildings were perfectly suited to 'alternative' uses: artists' studios, business premises and, above all, very agreeable dwellings – lofts, in the American sense. Whole rows of warehouses of almost medieval proportions have been transformed into attractive apartments with stunning views over water and sky, like these examples beside the Entrepotdok (the Warehouse Dock).

However, the architectural patrimony of Amsterdam is not limited to the impressive grandeur of the great houses of the Golden Age. You can also feel the pulse of history beating in the total silence that characterizes the little courtyards (*hofjes*) which abound in the old city. Each one is an oasis of peace encircled by identical small houses, living dolls' houses with their little gardens. The pearl of the *hofjes* is the Begijnhof (Court of the Beguines), squeezed between the Historical Museum (a former orphanage) and the Spui – a retiring little square of matchless charm. Here the visitor feels a certain awkwardness, as if he were intruding into someone's private life, although in theory he is still on the public highway. This sensation of embarrassment is simply the expression of the proper respect inspired by the Beguines and the *hofjes*. The voice is lowered and the attention is naturally attracted to small details, to inscriptions and reliefs, ornamentation and everyday objects – such as a half-door which, in the context of the little courtyard, suddenly takes on an affecting historical meaning.

Brick, wrought iron and oxidized bronze are materials to which Amsterdam architecture of the turn of the century assigned an expressive role. A detail of the roof of the Tuschinski cinema shows the exuberance of its style (facing page), while a lamp-post designed by H.P. Berlage stands in the Beursplein beside Berlage's Stock Exchange (left).

During my walks around the city I sometimes find myself talking to some of the monuments. I have conversations with them. In the Reguliersbreestraat (Broad Street of the Regular Clergy), for example, I never fail to pause for a moment to contemplate two cinemas built almost opposite each other, the Cineac and the Tuschinski. The Cineac has greater need of my concern, for this flower of 'modern construction' designed in 1934 by the architect Jan Duiker is dreadfully run down and neglected. The white walls, now greyish, are crumbling and the films shown there now are hardly art cinema.

Opposed to it, in both the spatial and the figurative sense, is the Tuschinski cinema (architect H.L. de Jong, 1918–1921), that monument of Art Deco flaunting an exotic luxuriance unheard-of in the Netherlands, which still accommodates 'gala premières' in the Hollywood tradition. The festive, phantasmagoric interior, where red and black predominate and whose every square inch seems to be drawn and painted on with particular care, forms a gigantic picture which glows with warmth, closing in on the visitor with the softness of velvet. In Amsterdam, the Tuschinski is the magical climax of that decadent turn-of-the-century style which is known variously as Art Nouveau (in the French- and English-speaking countries), Jugendstil (in Germany and Austria) or Slaolie ('salad oil' – derived from a work by Jan Tooroop, *Delftsche Slaolie*, which typified the period – in The Netherlands). Het Witte Huis (The White House, 1901) is the most rigorous example of this style. This building standing on the corner of the Singel (Moat), the Raadhuisstraat (Town Hall Street) and the Spuistraat (Sluice Street) already prefigures the modern architecture of the twentieth century, and it was a particularly inspired decision to integrate it, after a complete restoration, at the 'prow' of a new

The Tuschinski cinema possesses without question the most jubilant interior decoration in the whole city, giving exuberant expression to the spirit of the Roaring Twenties, of the true stars, of Clark Gable and Greta Garbo. The foyer carpet, a minor miracle, has recently been entirely rewoven by hand, following the original designs, having suffered irreparable damage from having cigarette butts stamped out on it for some seventy years.

48

The Scheepvaarthuis (Shipping House) marks the glorious apotheosis of the expressionistic style known as the Amsterdam School. The building was constructed in 1916, designed by J.M. van der Mey with the assistance of the architects M. de Klerk and P.L. Kramer. Many first-rank artists collaborated on the interior decoration of this monument of sculptural architecture. Since shipping no longer formed a major part of the city's activities, it was the municipal transport service that took over this secular cathedral.

Like the Beurs van Berlage, the Scheepvaarthuis is conceived as a whole. Inside – in the hall or the grand staircase – or out, a minutely detailed stylistic treatment is lavished on the smallest corner and the least important intermediate surface. It is a symphony of architecture which plays on all materials – brick, stone, cast iron, brass, stained glass.

building in amazing pale colours designed by Theo Bosch and built between 1978 and 1984, the P.C. Hooftgebouw (P.C. Hooft Building), which is home to the Literature Faculty of the University of Amsterdam.

H.P. Berlage's Beurs (Stock Exchange, 1903) is a spectacular monument of vast dimensions which also sits on the fence between the wearily imitative style of the nineteenth century and the modern architecture of the twentieth.

From an architectural point of view the Beurs is the most interesting monument in the whole of Amsterdam. I pass in front of it at least once a week and often go in. On these occasions I always give the massive timber doors a pat and run my finger along the light-red brick, that incomparable Dutch brick made by baking the rich clay taken from the verges of our river-banks. Brick is the building material that gives Amsterdam its distinctive look, instantly recognizable to anyone. All the architecture of H.P. Berlage (1856–1934) is made of brick inside and out. Brick is equally indissociable from the neo-gothic constructions of P.J.H. Cuypers (1827–1921), the Catholic builder of churches such as the Vondelkerk, but also creator of the Centraal Station and the Rijksmuseum – monuments without which the city would not seem itself – as well as the Bijenkorf (Beehive) department store. From the point of view of stylistic history I have always been amazed that this building, so traditional and classical in its formal vocabulary, was erected ten years after the Beurs. It seems to symbolize a reaction against the storm of criticism provoked by the earlier building. The Bijenkorf reasserted the imitative styles of the nineteenth century that the Beurs had so radically rejected.

The high point of brick architecture comes with the creations of the Amsterdam School, a

In 1903, the young Queen Wilhelmina opened Berlage's Stock Exchange on the Damrak. This great revolutionary monument, then known as the Koopmansbeurs (Commercial Exchange), was greeted by a wave of criticism: this bare, cheerless factory, this monstrous creation, sneered the city. Little by little, however, the public became used to modern lines, but only to those inspired by classical models, to the *Gesamtkunstwerk*, to that total work of art in which Berlage has brought together poets, painters, sculptors and master glaziers; and the new Beurs became a symbol of the passage from the imitative styles of the 19th century, in which decoration masked the structure, to undisguised modern architecture. The former hall of the Koopmansbeurs, placed under the protection of the statue of Mercury, is used nowadays for cultural activities and exhibitions. The rest of the building provides rehearsal rooms and concert halls for the Nederlands Filharmonisch Orkest (Netherlands Philharmonic Orchestra).

style that belongs to the huge blocks of flats built in the interwar years. It is a veritable symphony in brick, *trompe-l'oeil* architecture, decoration fit for a theatre or a masked ball, so many tools at the service of an idealistic conception of the aesthetic education of the labouring masses. On Prins Hendrikkade (Prince Hendrik's Quay) the Scheepvaarthuis (Shipping House) of 1913–1916, built by J.M. van der Mey, M. de Klerk and P. Kramer, both marks the beginning of and symbolizes the 'decorative architecture' of the Amsterdam School. With the apartment blocks of the Spaarndam quarter and the South Amsterdam Expansion Plan conceived in 1917 by Berlage, aesthetic idealism was bringing its big guns into action.

Today's visitor, walking through these districts that stand hidden well back from the main arteries – these pure products of the generous ideals of the twenties – feels bewildered, lost in time and in history. Look at the doors, the letter-boxes, the entrance-ways and above all the sheer theatricality of the tiled roofs: the impresario has left nothing to chance. And in fact the greater part of his twirling chorus-line of brick and red tiles still provides housing for workers, nowadays almost all immigrants.

There is one picture that I shall never forget. It appeared before me during a walk through this dream-like Spaarndam district to the west of the Centraal Station. I was keeping to the Hembrugstraat side, gazing up at the most famous piece of architecture of the Amsterdam School, the two blocks of brick flats designed in 1918 by Michel de Klerk which lean towards each other in a confidential way and celebrate their meeting in a veritable eruption of red tiles. Right in the middle of this architecture, which expresses an almost religious exaltation but whose modest dimensions exude a sort of rustic charm, a little

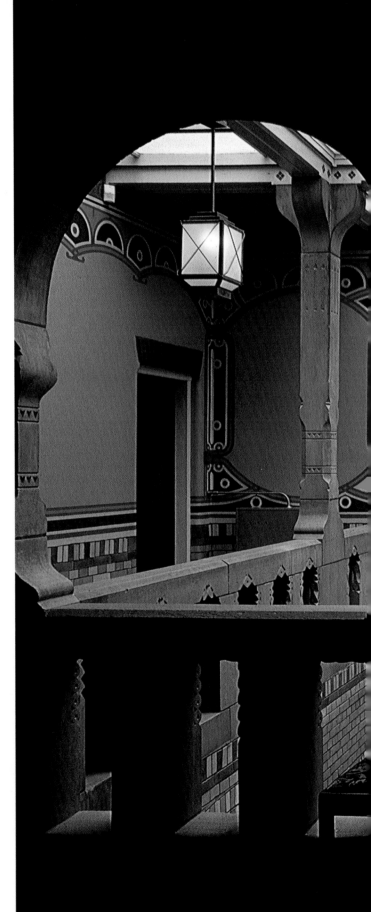

H.P. Berlage, architect, designer and town planner, left an indelible mark on Amsterdam. Apart from the Stock Exchange, his prolific drawing-board produced office buildings, dozens of blocks of flats and the famous expansion plan for Amsterdam South, the Nieuw Zuid. In 1899 he designed a headquarters on Henri Polaklaan for one of the country's oldest trade unions, the ANDB (General Netherlands Diamond Workers' Union) – a building better known by its nickname De Burcht van Berlage (Berlage's Fortress), in reference to its powerful simplicity in the use of brick. It is also sometimes said to have the look of an Italian *palazzo*, which is typical of Berlage's work. Above and opposite, the great staircase of this fortress palace, which now houses the Vakbondsmuseum (Trades Union Museum).

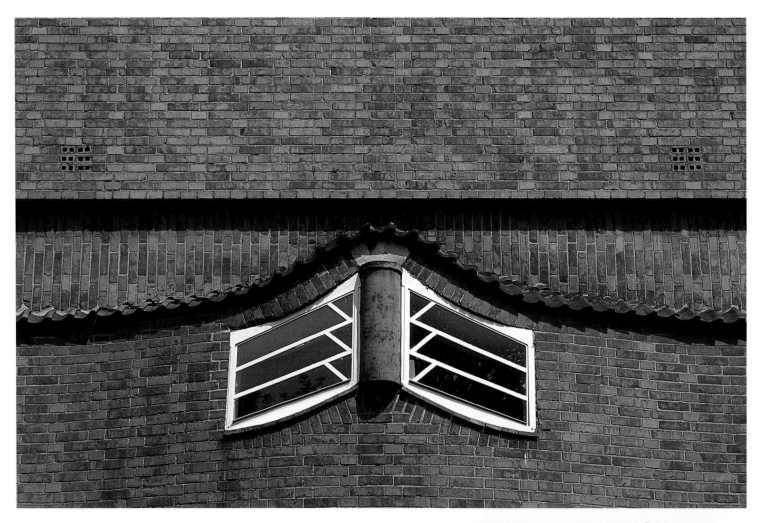

Lyricism in brick. Nowhere else in the world have architects shown such imagination in the use of brick. Starting with the idea that working people should be able to enjoy an environment of a high cultural standard to compensate them for often inhuman working conditions, the socially committed architects of the Amsterdam School composed symphonies in brick of which these pages offer a few brief snatches. In the easiest and most natural way, the new immigrant proletariat has succeeded the native Amsterdammers in these brick quarters that are so typical of the great city.

round diamond-paned window stands open. A Moslem woman is leaning out of it, her veil a white patch against the red tiles which begin, at this point, very close to the ground. And she is cleaning one by one, with methodical slowness, all the little window-panes so typical of the unique style of the Amsterdam School. I preserve a mental photograph of the scene, the most precious of my whole collection.

Great numbers of bricks of all colours, tiny windows framed in white. The Amsterdam School is a veritable open-air museum, and some of its finest exhibits are here in the Spaarndam district.

INTERIORS

Amsterdam interiors reflect
the state of mind, the moral attitudes
and the remarkable imagination of the Dutch.
They vie in inventiveness to merge quiet
comfort with refined opulence, residence
with warehouse. They are daring magicians
in a new art of living, as much in the
restricted resources of traditional
dwellings as in the vastness of the
converted spaces that they have
made their homes.

The Dutch, who according to an English humorist invented private life, also created a type of house which illustrates at the same time their mental attitude, their morality and their imagination. The aristocrats and rich merchants of Amsterdam vied with each other in finding ways of combining a comfortable life-style with the evidence of wealth, but like good Calvinists they rejected useless luxury and arrogant pride.

Amsterdammers have a subtle taste for paradox, which often tempts the foreigner to see their attitudes as a series of contradictions: thus their liking for balance and moderation has never got in the way of their enjoyment of good living, banquets, lavish celebrations and domestic comfort. Similarly, their preference for openness in their private lives would seem to have found an ideal expression in their homes, thrown wide open to the outside world – except that the passer-by who at first thought he could see everything that was going on very soon realizes that they are in fact impenetrably opaque. The Amsterdammers' passion for speculation was as much intellectual as financial and they pursued the law of opposites with enthusiasm: nothing is what it seems and the most lucid appearance often conceals some mysterious enigma.

Although architecture springs from aesthetic principles, it is constrained from the outset by practical considerations. Amsterdam is the smallest of the great European cities; its space had to be won from the marshes and was therefore used sparingly. Here, very early, the civic laws codified building practice and a number of special features of the town houses are the brilliant product of necessity: houses cannot have a broad façade since the street frontage is limited, therefore they have greater depth than breadth; since the northern light and a certain moral

NOBLE HOUSES

—

The remarkable red and white brick façade of the Bartolotti House enhances the waterside frontage of the Herengracht (above). Within, the sumptuous decorations of the Golden Age have been trimmed of superfluous ornamentation, retaining only the essential elements of a historic setting which is at the same time both opulent and austere. Framed by woodwork in mahogany and teak – much in vogue in the Golden Age, as was anything imported from the colonies – a beautiful late-17th-century white marble fountain is incorporated in the wall of the principal reception room (opposite).

attitude require a house to be open to the outside, it was not long before the front wall pierced by huge windows was created – a system which also had the merit of reducing the weight of the building on terrain so unstable that, before any construction work could take place, numerous piles had to be driven into the ground. For the same reason brick was preferred to stone, as was sandstone for window embrasures, since this was comparatively light and lent itself to the rich carved decoration that characterized local taste at the beginning of the Golden Age that made Holland an island of prosperity, tolerance and freedom in a Europe torn by endless wars and cataclysms of every kind.

The rich of Amsterdam included a love of houses among their many passions, and the works of Jan Steen, Nicolaes Maes, Pieter de Hooch and dozens of lesser painters demonstrate how they liked to be portrayed in their own homes, even in the most commonplace situations. Inventories made after their death reveal that they often spent as much on decoration as they did on building or buying their houses.

All through the seventeenth century the decorative arts flourished in Amsterdam, craftsmen – often driven from their own countries by religious intolerance or the ravages of war – flocked in, and imports of mirrors, lacquerwork, silks and porcelain rapidly increased, while local workshops proliferated and, inspired by the objects arriving from all corners of the world, very quickly attained a remarkably high degree of skill.

The residence of an Amsterdam patrician was not only a peaceful family refuge but was also meant to mirror the brilliance of a financial success which often manifested itself more in the opulence of interior design than by the richness of the exterior. This contrasts with the ways of

other great mercantile republics, particularly Venice before the influence of Palladio made itself felt during the second half of the seventeenth century.

All along the canals, and observing a subtle hierarchy which put the Herengracht (the Gentlemen's Canal) in the front rank – although it was the most austere with its almost religious insistence on keeping the façades on an alignment that would not interfere with mercantile activity – these splendid residences arose, the most immediately perceptible legacy of that age of prosperity. Every merchant wanted his house, which also did duty as his warehouse, to be as sumptuous as his means permitted. These façades which give rhythm to the quays along the canals are like so many proclamations of prosperity, decorated with heraldic devices carved in the stone, with richly elaborate gables, and some also adorned with a bust of the proprietor.

The Bartolotti House on the Herengracht, now partly occupied by one of the great musicians of our time, is undoubtedly the most impressive achievement of its period. Hendrick de Keyser, sculptor and prolific architect of the early Golden Age, to whom were entrusted many important state and city commissions, was chosen to carry out this prestigious building contract in 1617 by Willem van den Heuvel, a rich merchant and administrator of the United East India Company who had taken the surname of his Bolognese father-in-law in return for the promise that he would inherit the widow's vast fortune. The architect circumvented the requirement to respect the 'royal measure' of one *kavel* (the standard tenement) of 7.35 metres (24 feet) wide by 60 metres (almost 200 feet) deep by joining together two *kavels* along the bend of the quay. He created a magnificent, very Italianate façade,

The immaculate stucco decorations of the entrance hall of the Bartolotti House depict mythological scenes (above). This superb plasterwork, which is to be found in most of the patrician mansions and grand country houses, was introduced into The Netherlands by some notable Italian craftsmen.

In the kitchen, the most convivial room in the house, where blue-painted woodwork frames the Soignies stone sink, an adorable white-marble Cupid has dropped off to sleep (opposite). There is also one of those pewter jugs so dear to the famous still-life painters Pieter Claesz. and Willem Claesz. Heda.

richly decorated but of great structural rigour, certainly The Netherlands' finest example of Renaissance style. In the seventeenth century the Bartolotti House contained an impressive collection of paintings and was packed with fine furniture and decorations: the master bedroom had twelve paintings hanging on its walls and there were seven in one of the servants' rooms, while several rooms were hung with tooled and gilded leather and with mirrors – extremely costly at that time.

Contrary to custom, Hendrick de Keyser planned the main reception rooms on the ground floor rather than the first. Grouped round the entrance hall, painted bright blue and paved with grey marble, they comprised a series of rooms sumptuously decorated with carved teak and mahogany by a pupil of Daniel Marot, and with plaster ceilings of a creamy whiteness, the most striking of which was the 'great room' intended for receptions and parties. Today a calmer atmosphere prevails, and while the original richness of decoration survives – notably some superb plasterwork of mythological subjects as well as a staircase built about a century later than the house – it is enhanced by many antique musical instruments which testify to the present owner's love of music. These are more conducive to meditation and contemplation than to the animated spirit of the perpetual festivities that once enlivened the scene. The numerous reception rooms now seem to have been abandoned and it is in the false 'basement' so typical of Amsterdam houses, reached by a few steps down from the quay but in fact on a level with the garden at the back of the house, that the musician's family gathers. In this warm, brightly lit atmosphere everyone gravitates towards the kitchen, for that is the room that has always been the centre of Dutch family life. At a time when

the functions of the various rooms were rather vaguely defined, and when a bedroom might also serve as a reception room, the kitchen was always the most welcoming and the warmest room in the house. It was not thought improper to receive guests there even among the higher class of merchants who were in some ways over-zealous in their observance of a way of life modelled on that of the aristocracy, and the lady of the house would cheerfully engage in domestic activities at the same time as entertaining her guests. These days everyone in the Bartolotti House lives in the bright, colourful kitchen with its traditional sink in blue Soignies stone, its cupboards laden with crockery and its vast fireplace lined with Delft-ware tiles, and it is there that music is played.

Paradoxically, the best-preserved house of the Golden Age is actually outside town. Hoorn, the busiest port on the Zuiderzee until it was cut off from the sea by the construction of a dyke to create new polders, still has some magnificent period houses. A house built in 1624 and now occupied by the art historian Johannes de Visser gives a clear idea of the domestic background of a shipbuilder in Holland's heyday. The entrance door is divided horizontally like a stable door and flanked by windows with small leaded panes. The floor is still paved with *pavluizen*, those little glazed earthenware tiles that are seen in so many paintings of Dutch interiors. A small spiral staircase leads up to the shipbuilder's very plain office, contrasting sharply with the next-door house, purchased twenty years later, which the owner chose to decorate with all the baroque fantasy typical of that sumptuous period, eager for pleasure and parties, when the brightest of colours found favour. Dutch houses are far from always being like those depicted in paintings of the time. Austerity, simplicity, a liking for empty

The entrance to this house in Hoorn still has the pentagram intended to ward off evil spirits (top).

The hallway, paved with old *pavluizen*, has an opening cut in the door panelling, through which the shipbuilder could keep a close eye on deliveries. The handsome *toogkast* or carved cupboard on the left is a typically Dutch piece of the 17th century (above).

Beneath a mirror in a Flemish walnut frame, the superb Frisian console table dates from 1688 (opposite).

spaces – all that certainly did exist, but it is not the whole story and does not convey the great variety, rich in surprises and allurements, that characterized the period.

Now let us return to Amsterdam, a city abounding in new and second-hand bookshops. In the house of the founder of the *Bibliotheca Philosophica Hermetica* on the Bloemgracht (Flower Canal), we come into an atmosphere of intellectual concentration. He is happy to open his library to lovers of erudite works or rare editions of mystics – Holland was one of the centres of esoteric writing – or anything pertaining to alchemy and secret societies. In a haven of peace that houses four hundred manuscripts (more than half of them dating from before 1600) and fifteen thousand books, this refined man of letters from an active business background has created an almost anachronistic study where the bustle of the outside world is barely heard, and it is quite hard to realize that the room is far more recent than the house that contains it. Its furnishings are simple but perfectly in keeping – a carved oak cupboard decorated with three statues symbolizing biblical virtues such as was customarily presented to young brides on their wedding day; a seventeenth-century clock by Pieter Klock of Amsterdam; a cabinet by Erik van Rijswijck; and a table covered with a tapestry of flowers and leaves, such as you often see in interior scenes painted at that period – all these perfectly re-create a way of life that seems timeless. There is not much light in the house with its small windows, as was usual up to the first quarter of the seventeenth century, and it is lit by one of those brass chandeliers, to be found in both churches and private houses, whose form has changed little over the years – but this one is of uncommon size and workmanship. A tranquil

The Delft plate with symmetrical monogram (below) dates from the last quarter of the 17th century.

On the table (bottom) have been set an elegant René Lalique decanter, a snuff-box, a typical biscuit box and some Dutch glassware.

A portrait of the children of the mayor of Zwolle, painted in 1668 by Joanna Vergouwen, dominates the drawing-room. The bunches of ostrich feathers in *trompe l'oeil* marble vases, the cast-iron Napoleon III day-bed and the satin and zebra-striped cushions create a carefully studied effect of apparent disarray (right).

Johannes de Visser has refurbished the neighbouring house, turning for inspiration to the style for which the great French-born architect Daniel Marot was famous in the early 18th century. Over the fireplace are carved-wood brackets for displaying porcelain, based on sketches by Jean Berain. The chairs covered in Utrecht velvet, the silk-brocade table-cloth and the 'thousand-colour' carpet woven at the great Deventer factory in the province of Overijssel combine to create a cheerfully baroque effect (above).

silence encourages introspection, broken only by the sound of wood crackling on the hearth of the vast fireplace decorated with earthenware tiles from factories pre-dating those of Delft, depicting towns in northern Holland.

The people of Amsterdam even manage to satisfy their taste for tranquility in places that are open to the public, such as the Amstelkring Museum. This was created in 1888 in a house built in 1663 on the Oudezijds Voorburgwal (Old Side Inner City Wall), which had at first contained a Catholic church known as Het Hert (The Stag) in its attic and extending through the adjoining houses. Catholicism was officially banned but in practice allowed, as long as it was discreet, at that time when intolerance reigned throughout Europe. About ten of these secret chapels have survived in the whole city. This is the best preserved and the most moving, and is known by the rather naive name of Ons' Lieve Heer op Solder (Our Lord in the Attic) conferred on it in the nineteenth century. To the observant visitor, however, the whole house bears witness to the continued presence of Catholicism in Amsterdam, whether by the portraits of governors of charities or by religious scenes typifying the Counter-Reformation aesthetic, such as the Annunciation, scenes of the Passion, the Evangelists or the Trinity. Passing through the very beautiful, sometimes richly decorated, rooms of this house it is impossible to feel oneself in a sacred place, even though its existence was common knowledge from the first and was always perfectly acceptable through a sort of *modus vivendi* that typified the spirit of this Calvinist country. The house is a world apart from the city, and the spirit of a community still breathes in its labyrinth of corridors and staircases and in its bedrooms with their built-in beds, where the magic lives on and time seems to stand still.

The founder of the *Bibliotheca Philosophica Hermetica* welcomes bibliophiles from all over the world in an authentic 17th-century setting in the Jordaan. His passion for rare antiquarian books is demonstrated by the volumes lying on the table, which include a St Augustine dated 1470, an *Imitation of Jesus Christ* bound in red with its original box, and the famous Dutch Book of Hours illuminated in 1491 by a master known, from his manner of painting, as the 'Master of the Dark Eyes' (right).

Stained-glass panels in the original windows depict naval battle scenes (above).

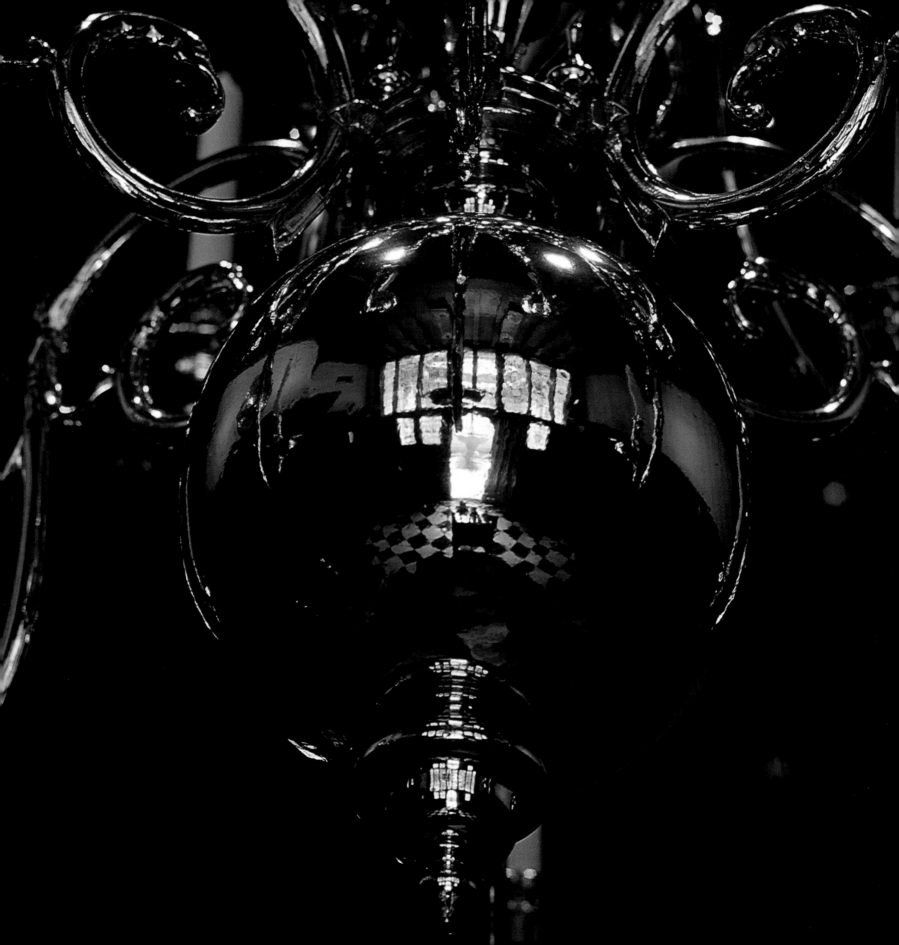

The characteristic chequer-board flagstones of a 17th-century interior are reflected in the gleaming brass of one of those monumental chandeliers of the period, such as appear in the paintings of Pieter de Hooch and which are still frequently to be found in churches (opposite).

Another perfect 17th-century décor, that of a little house in the Oudezijds Voorburgwal which is now a museum. On the first floor in the 'great room', a carved oak table with characteristic bulbous legs is set off by the Delft tiles and twisted columns of an enormous fireplace (above).

Friendly and welcoming, the kitchen where the owner receives her friends is a good example of the convivial atmosphere of Dutch kitchens with its floor paved in Carrara marble, its huge fireplace and antique pump-action taps (left).

The Golden Age was never confined to a single aesthetic. Throughout this time of prosperity merchants and aristocrats, vying in magnificence, constantly discovered new talents and encouraged innovative ideas. Following Hendrick de Keyser, who died in 1621, Philips Vingboons – who often worked with his brother Justus Vingboons, the designer of the most successful work of neo-classicism, the Trippenhuis on the Kloveniersburgwal – is the most attractive representative of that generation of architects who achieved early success by making use of forms that were spreading all over Europe but which found a particular national expression here. More extrovert, skilfully using the effect of perspective to enlarge the actual space and showing a sensuous enjoyment of ornamentation, this architecture was made to seduce – and seduce it did, very rapidly. In 1638 Vingboons, only thirty years old, was engaged by the magistrate Michiel Pauw to build his new house on the Herengracht. This looks to us today like a traditional Amsterdam building but was in fact highly innovative, being the first to include the 'neck gable', a particularly sophisticated variation on an ancient theme. The gable of the narrow town house was often the only place where the architect could give rein to his imagination; soaring heavenwards, more decorative than useful, it served the same function for the architect as his coat-of-arms did for the owner: it demonstrated his temperament, his taste and his ambitions. In this most elegant quarter of the city, which from its very beginning symbolized success, Vingboons broke away from the standard cramped proportions to design a dwelling of vast dimensions with a monumental staircase whose function was subordinate to aesthetic considerations, and with a series of rooms on the French model, suggesting a way of

The theatre museum (Nederlands Theater Instituut) has been installed in the house next door to the Bartolotti House, of which indeed it occupies a part. Inside, along with the magnificent stucco decoration by the sculptor Jan van Logteren, the visitor can enjoy an impressive collection of costumes, model sets and scenery (opposite).

The perfect spiral of the staircase rises in a single flight from cellar to attic (above).

life more intimate than in the past, which was to become the fashion for an entire generation. However, since it is in the nature of fashion to be superseded by new fashions, in 1730 Michiel Pauw's successors set about a new decorative scheme, leaving the house as we see it today. Alas, Vingboons's legendary staircase has disappeared, replaced by a more sophisticated spiral model that rises from cellar to eaves in one continuous flight, contrary to the usual practice of interrupting it on the first floor – the reception level – to continue to the upper levels with a lower standard of workmanship. Nowadays it is Jan van Logteren's superb stuccowork that constitutes the mansion's primary, celebrated attraction. The virtuoso artist plays brilliant games of *trompe l'oeil* with false or truncated perspectives and a vast range of ornamental devices to dazzle the visitor, even creating false doors for the sake of a symmetry which he chooses to break only a few feet further on. Ceilings by Jacob de Wit, a master of mythological scenes in *grisaille* – often including little angels nicknamed '*witjes*' in his honour – and by the French-born landscape artist Isaac de Moucheron, overdoors and numerous allegorical decorations, walls hung with embossed and gilded Cordovan leather, all add to the impression of an opulence which firmly turns its back on the notion of puritanism which we tend automatically, and often mistakenly, to associate with the Dutch spirit. This building, now the Netherlands Theatre Institute, has relinquished its seventeenth-century delusions of grandeur to house the often unexpected, and always touching, relics of the art of theatrical illusion.

As neo-classical taste began to assert itself, the houses of Amsterdam returned to a certain austerity – at least in their façades if not always in their interiors. The Van Loon house on the

Keizersgracht is a good example of this, famous as much for its quality as for the fact that, now converted into a museum, it is one of the few town houses open to visitors, and the turbulent history of its successive proprietors bears witness to the ways of high society in past times.

Built in 1671 by Adriaan Dorsman, like its neighbouring twin, it is typical of that austere architect, sometimes rather stiff and strongly influenced by Jacob van Campen, who was chosen in preference to Philips Vingboons in the competition to build the Town Hall, which since the brief reign of Louis Bonaparte has been the Royal Palace. The Keizersgracht was, like its contemporaries the Herengracht (more elegant) and the Prinsengracht (quieter because farther from the centre), among the areas most favoured by the rich burghers of the Golden Age. It was therefore quite natural that Jeremias van Raey, whose fortune had just seen a rapid increase, should decide to take up residence there, carefully instructing the architect to set his coat-of-arms – a stag couchant – on the balustrade of the sandstone façade between statues of the gods and goddesses of war, fire, earth and wisdom, while his monogram was to constitute the central decorative motif of the balconies.

Demonstrating a taste for the classical marked by the cosmopolitan spirit of the age, the decorative scheme of the house eventually occupied by the free-spending La Fargue-Sanders couple might just as easily fit in on the Faubourg Saint-Germain in Paris as on the Keizersgracht. In spite of its elegance, the house rather lacks personality. Paradoxically, the finest decorative elements come from other places, such as the panoramas brought in 1970 from the palace of Drakestein or Gerard de Lairesse's wonderful *grisailles* of the very early seventeenth century, brought by Jonas Witsen, Baron Straalman, who

Behind the canal houses there are often long gardens hidden from view, hemmed in by former coach-houses (*koetshuizen*). Pierre Audi, Director of the Muziektheater, lives in the one belonging to the Van Loon house. On the first floor of this elegant little building, whose neo-classical pediment gives it rather the look of a Greek temple, *trompe-l'oeil* windows have been painted. The garden has been redesigned, based on a 17th-century bird's-eye view (above).

The Van Loon Museum offers an exceptional chance to explore a patrician canal-side house with its 18th-century decoration perfectly preserved. The collection of portraits tells the family's story. In the hall, hanging above an 18th-century ebony and teak trunk from the United East India Company, a large painting signed Jan Miense Molenaer depicts the wedding in 1637 of Willem van Loon and Margaretha Bas (right).

lived here from 1842 to 1860. This was some twenty years before the house was bought by Hendrick van Loon, whose descendants, now represented by the archaeologist Maurits van Loon, decided to turn their house into a foundation and museum after extensive restoration to re-create its appearance of the late eighteenth/early nineteenth century. This old Dutch family, originally from Loon near 's-Hertogenbosch where they owned mills, was associated with the creation of the United East India Company; the two Moors' heads incorporated into their coat-of-arms in 1600 are a reminder of this.

The walls of this charming residence, which are largely taken up by numerous portraits of the Van Loon family (who still live here), also enclose some attractive heirlooms, among them a lovely collection of old silver and a service of Amstel porcelain of the mid-eighteenth century comprising 240 pieces, which are on view in a dining-room lit by a rare and magnificent chandelier in carved wood which was originally covered in silver leaf. But more than anything else it is the serene, almost joyous, atmosphere which fills the rooms of the handsome suite opening directly on to the garden that gives a sense of a most enticing way of life. At the bottom of the garden a building typically neo-classical in taste contained the stables and the coachmen's lodging. Opening on both the little garden and the Kerkstraat (Church Street), it is undoubtedly a work of Dorsman. Progressively modified, this utilitarian building took on the temple-like aspect seen today, with its two statues of Bacchus and Flora in niches while Apollo stands over the entrance. This is probably the best place in which to take the measure of what these houses were once like, with gardens which, despite their narrowness, had the look of parks and for which a subtle play of geometry and perspective was created to make the space seem

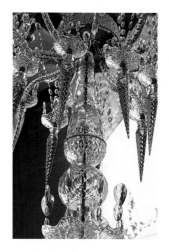

A detail of the 18th-century English rock-crystal chandelier which lights the staircase (top). Woven into the interlacing pattern of the handsome balustrade are the names 'vHagen' and 'Trip', commemorating Abraham van Hagen and his wife Catharina Trip who lived here in the 18th century (above).
　The little sitting-room (*tuinkamer*, literally 'garden room') built on to the house in 1870, its walls hung with toile de Jouy, was used as a summer dining-room (opposite).

larger. Balancing the façade, the garden is like its mirror image, somewhat softened but just as rigorously organized.

The Van Brienen House on the Herengracht is like a dream of a Palladian villa come to town with its perfect classical façade of sandstone designed in 1728 by Frédéric Blanchard, a French architect who had taken refuge in Amsterdam. Its interior is richly decorated with marble panelling, plasterwork and a brightly lit stairway with a lemonwood handrail, and much of its fame is due to the painted room executed by Dirk Dalens and Antonie Elliger in the style of Pynacker. The fashion for rooms decorated with large scenes painted on canvas and set in the woodwork began about the second third of the seventeenth century and was an instant success. These large-scale paintings of panoramic landscapes – Dutch or exotic – with allegorical or moral scenes could also represent the activities of the master of the house in a stylized way, and demonstrate his wealth. But the Van Brienen House possesses in its inner courtyard another element specific to Amsterdam houses, though it has disappeared in many cases. This was a decorative motif carved in wood, resembling an organ console and running right up the façade, on which the statues of a woman carrying a censer, and a stork, symbolized maternal love and filial piety. The privies were concealed at the sides of this woodwork. At the bottom of the garden an arbour – built like the tea-houses of country mansions – allowed people to take the air and something to drink while enjoying the view of the 'French' garden with its box-bordered alleys.

The Van Brienen House, which since 1918 has been the home of the Vereniging Hendrick de Keyser (Hendrick de Keyser Society) dedicated

to preserving the old houses of the Netherlands, was built in the seventeenth century and renovated in the eighteenth by the Rutgers family. It is a perfect example of a house built for the dual purpose of trading and residence: its warehouses in the basement (near the quay) to facilitate loading, as well as above the first floor, surround the rooms dedicated to domestic comfort, which generally look out on the garden while those giving on to the quayside are kept as offices. This arrangement, widely used throughout the city, indicates the kind of speculative trading involved, in which speed of delivery was of prime importance.

The summerhouse at the bottom of the garden of the Van Brienen House (which contains the offices of the Hendrick de Keyser Society) has been made into a tea-room for visitors (below).

A statue of filial piety watches reassuringly over the well-being of the occupants from the well-lit central courtyard (opposite).

The Mayor of Amsterdam still has an official residence on the Herengracht at his disposal for entertaining guests in a style that befits his office. This mansion was built in 1671 by un unknown architect for Paulus Godin, a merchant of Huguenot extraction who was administrator to the United East India Company. Unusually, instead of the normal entrance steps it had a short flight of stairs framed between two stone columns, with side doors leading to the warehouses. In about 1790 a descendant of Paulus Godin engaged Abraham van der Hart, one of Amsterdam's leading exponents of the classical school and architect of the Maagdenhuis (Girls'

On the first floor of the Van Brienen House, facing the garden, the splendid painted room is used as a sitting-room. The landscapes are the work of Dirk Dalens, while the overmantel and the ceiling were painted by Antonie Helliger (right).

The Gobelins tapestries on the walls of the Mayor of Amsterdam's dining-room were installed in 1804 and are in perfect harmony with the late-Louis XVI chairs (opposite). The room also has doors carved with musical instruments and a score on which the first five bars of the Marseillaise can be deciphered.

Orphanage), to modify the mansion inside and out in order to bring it into line with current taste. While the façade was simply remodelled on a larger scale, which led to the disappearance of all the original ornamentation, the interior underwent a more profound transformation. Suppressing the warehouses to increase the space available for reception rooms and for accommodating a larger household, Van der Hart created a decorative scheme in the purest Louis XVI style – currently in vogue all over Europe. Rejecting all vernacular influence, this mansion became the prototype for a cosmopolitan style and embodied an economic shift from speculation in commodity trading to purely financial transactions. The woodwork is carved with classical designs, the chimneypieces, severe in design, are decorated with medallions representing classical mythology, the overdoors show allegorical scenes, and the Gobelins tapestries have coloured borders with motifs in the style of Berain. The proportions of the house, while generous, are still on a comfortably domestic scale and it was perfectly suited to its newly acquired function of welcoming municipal guests, at the same time giving them a sense of intimacy in the second-floor apartments where they stayed, from which they looked down on to a 'French' garden culminating in a summerhouse at the far end.

A gazebo stands at the bottom of the 'French' garden of the Mayor of Amsterdam's official residence (above).

The Louis XVI ballroom, lit by a majestic rock-crystal chandelier, is sumptuously decorated in gilt and plasterwork and has a white marble chimneypiece carved with mythological figures. Chubby little angels in *grisaille*, nicknamed *witjes* in honour of the painter Jacob de Wit who painted hundreds of them, adorn the overdoors (right).

If the great Amsterdam merchants always preferred to live in town close to the nerve-centre of their economic and political activity, it was because they represented a narrow oligarchy wielding a degree of power that often brought them into conflict with the princes of Orange-Nassau, whose power derived from a more popular base. The Batavian aristocracy for its part often kept up the tradition of residing in the country, thus preserving, at least symbolically, its function as the military defender of The Netherlands.

Duivenvoorde Castle, between Amsterdam and The Hague, whose earliest foundations date from 1226, exemplifies that way of life and its evolution. It was occupied from the first by the Van Wassenaer family, several of whom were very close to the princes of Orange, particularly Arend van Wassenaer, the son of the man who rebuilt the castle in its present form. He went to England with the Stadholder William III and married the daughter of the Earl of Portland. As a result of this royal patronage, he was able to call on Daniel Marot, a Huguenot who had fled from France, to rebuild the great ballroom. Marot had already built a number of patrician mansions in The Hague, where he introduced the fashion for a succession of rooms opening into each other. Later he took part in the rebuilding of the royal palace of Het Loo near Apeldoorn to the east of Amsterdam.

Duivenvoorde, where the main structure was built on the medieval foundations, was enlarged during the first third of the seventeenth century. Two wings framed a terrace overlooking an expanse of water, adorned with stone vases retrieved from the former 'French' garden. The castle, which combines the atmosphere of an aristocratic palace of the Golden Age with the

LIFE AT THE CASTLE

——

Through a tall window with rectangular glazing bars in the thick red-brick walls which give Muiden Castle its solidly defensive air, the characteristic shape of a monumental brass chandelier can be seen (above).

The symmetrical and elegant façade of Duivenvoorde Castle, built at the height of the Golden Age, looks down on the surface of its lake. The brickwork has been almost literally eaten away by the great rectangular-paned windows, which have been enlarged three times in the course of the castle's history (opposite).

more refined and comfortable charm of the eighteenth century, contains fine furniture and *objets d'art* together with a notable collection of Delft pottery, Chinese porcelain, many paintings, a Turkish bedroom of the kind favoured towards the end of the nineteenth century, and a library of old books. Duivenvoorde, which is like a sampler of all the most interesting achievements of Dutch craftsmanship, has the integrity that comes from having remained in the same family through seven centuries, until, that is, Baroness Ludolphine Schimmelpenninck van der Oye donated it to an association which undertook to conserve it and has in fact completely restored it.

Muiden Castle (Muiderslot), whose medieval austerity evokes the harshness of war rather than the pleasures of the countryside, rises beside the Vecht, which from the earliest times was a favoured recreation spot for the people of Amsterdam. This river, forming the strategic axis between Utrecht and the North Sea ports, was a determining factor in the economic life of Holland and control over it could send a whole region into economic decline, even one bristling with fortified castles. The forbidding Muiden Castle was built at the very beginning of the thirteenth century and completely remodelled from 1370 onwards, with the living quarters grouped round an interior courtyard. After playing a central role in resisting the Spaniards, it rejected the gods of war in favour of the arts of peace. Here lived the poet and dramatist Pieter Cornelisz. Hooft and round him gathered a literary circle fit to rival the intellectual refinements of the Hôtel de Rambouillet in Paris. The Muiderkring (Muiden Circle), which united the humanistic ideals of the Italian Renaissance with the liberal, tolerant spirit of Holland, brought

Duivenvoorde Castle contains some of the country's finest private collections. A covered jar of German origin and a collection of English glasses engraved in Holland in the 18th century testify to the superb reputation of the Dutch engravers, to whom glasses were sent from all over Europe to receive the benefit of their skills. Often unique, such glasses commemorated special events – weddings, christenings, travels – or sometimes they simply bear a family coat-of-arms (left).

A service of Loosdrecht porcelain displayed on a Louis XIV buffet is a reminder of the undeserved fate of that factory which, despite the fine quality of its products, could not stand up to French and English competition and had to close its doors in 1784 after only ten years' operation (left).

On a Louis XV marquetry commode, some Loosdrecht and Meissen pieces stand side by side with French biscuit porcelain figurines (above).

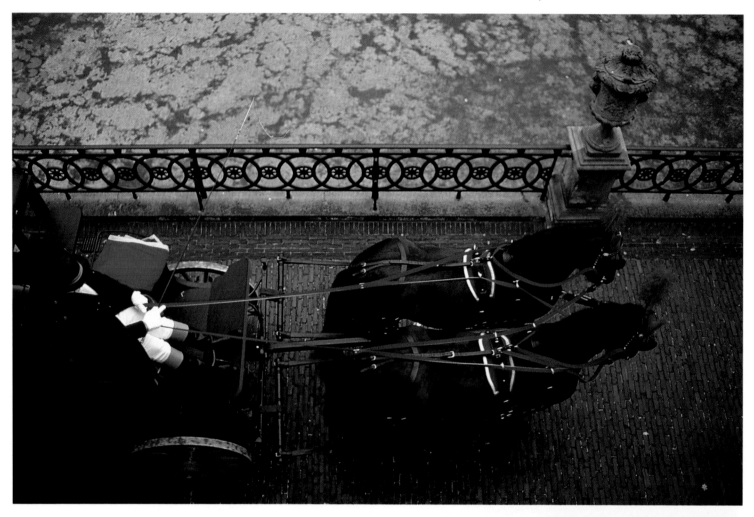

Duivenvoorde Castle, which now belongs to a foundation, can be hired for parties or ceremonies and is often used for wedding receptions (above).

The castle stands in an 'English' park which was badly damaged by bombing during the Second World War. The flanking bridges are ornamented with an extremely rare collection of stone vases (right).

Nothing has changed in the attic linen-room, from the rollers and mangles to the furniture painted 'fly blue', a colour that was supposed to repel flies. Such linen-rooms can also be seen in the wonderful dolls' houses, real miniatures of patrician mansions, in the Rijksmuseum or the Frans Hals Museum (opposite).

together such men of distinction as the great poet Joost van den Vondel, the composer Jan Pietersz. Sweelinck and the sage Constantijn Huygens, as well as the French philosopher Descartes. This community of learned minds open to all the arts and to all intellectual speculation had found in this rugged bastion an illustration of what Holland meant in that century of wars and intolerance: a fortress of liberty. After that period of glory, however, the castle fell into disuse until it was restored at the beginning of the present century, bringing back the authentic atmosphere of the Golden Age perhaps to a greater degree than any town mansion could, since the latter have usually undergone a whole series of modifications.

The garden at Muiden, classified and protected as part of the national heritage, has been faithfully restored to its appearance in Hooft's time. Conceived to a severely structured plan orientated on the axis of the castle and outlined with box hedges, it houses a collection of medicinal plants, dye-plants and aromatics in a brightly coloured mass that contrasts with the severity of its geometry, while a wonderful arbour of pleached limes inspired by Renaissance gardens stretches the length of the herb garden.

The portrait of the poet Pieter Cornelisz. Hooft, Muiden's most famous occupant, painted in 1629 by Michiel van Mierevelt, hangs over a 17th-century rent table with a stone top which enabled the rent-collector to test coins by the sound they made. The bench set in front of the fireplace tiled in blue Delft has a movable back, enabling people to sit with either faces or backs to the fire. On the other side of the hearth is a picture showing the group of friends who made up the Muiderkring.

Muiden Castle, flanked by great round towers, has retained its warlike aspect, although this is softened by the luxuriance of the garden. Following a plan typical of the period, the living quarters are arranged around a square courtyard (right).

An arched arbour with openings that allow the light through leads to the stone image of one of the muses of the Muiderkring (opposite).

The garden, reconstructed using the original plans, mixes all kinds of herbal plants in a delightful colour harmony framed by geometric box hedges (above).

The neighbouring Sypesteyn Castle breathes the same nostalgia for times past. It was built in 1911 on the site of a medieval fortress by Jonkheer C.H.C.A. van Sypesteyn, author of an important book on old gardens of The Netherlands. Apart from his writing, this energetic country gentleman dreamed up a moated mansion in the Renaissance style to house the extremely rich collections of old porcelain from Loosdrecht, Weesp and Amstel – pieces all the more rare because so often ignored in favour of Delftware – built up by several generations of his ancestors. He lacked the means to complete his mission, but nonetheless has bequeathed a fascinating museum of sculpture, arms, silverware, *objets d'art* and furniture.

The visitor enters the park through a little wooden door in an old stone wall to be confronted by a carpet of flowering bulbs backed by tall columns of clipped yews. The flowerbeds are famous for their beauty, with perennials and roses, edged by box hedges, leading towards a maze of beech and yew and on beyond the moat to a dense wood that holds out the promise of a lovely walk. Sypesteyn, a mad but calculated dream, though never fully realized, is more than just a curiosity. It represents the ultimate, anachronistic symbol of the Dutch people's attachment to their way of life.

In the dining-room of Sypesteyn Castle, the table, draped with an 18th-century damask table-cloth, is set with a marvellous service of Loosdrecht porcelain. On either side of the cabinet which contains Loosdrecht and Amstel porcelain are portraits of the founder of the Loosdrecht factory and his wife. The bust of Hortense de Beauharnais is a reminder of the French occupation under Napoleon.

Behind ditches and moats, majestic blue wrought-iron railings guard access to Sypesteyn's park, where beds of flowers and a wild wood bloom around a box maze. Once a week, a group of volunteers comes to keep up the park (right and opposite).

Its relative newness – it was built in 1911 – does not prevent Sypesteyn Castle from being a remarkable museum. Built in the purest 16th-century style, it contains some superb collections (left).

When night falls and the city lights go on, Amsterdam is reflected in the still water of the canals and the walker can gaze endlessly at the inverted image of the rows of harmonious façades.

Is it the vertigo of repetition that has stirred the Amsterdammers to such enthusiasm for collecting? These heirs to a famous mercantile tradition very early converted a simple taste for accumulation to a passion for beautiful things. The city is a closed universe irrigated by alluvial streams of countless objects imported from all over the world, and here the collector's mania finds the ideal soil in which to flourish. His own collection is but one among many to which he has access and which further excite his thirst, fuelling his dream of the unique find – the ultimate goal of a collector's life, a heady but frustrating ambiguity in the search for beauty.

In the library of the *achterhuis* (rear premises) of the house on the Keizersgracht, built in 1640 and rebuilt many times, where Ronald de Leeuw lives, first editions of Byron share the shelves with a highly important collection of the works of the Dutch poet and dramatist Joost van den Vondel, who has often been considered equal to his contemporary Rembrandt in importance, though there is more of Rubens in his taste for vast compositions, virtuosity and abundance. Amsterdammers do not appear to hold it against this man of paradox that, though born a Protestant, he became Holland's greatest Catholic poet. They are devoted to him, and have named a magnificent nineteenth-century park after him.

On the ground floor of this very simple house the sitting-room and kitchen give directly on to a little garden of clipped box designed by Michael van Gessel. The proportions of the sitting-room make it the ideal place to enjoy lounging about at

A PASSION FOR COLLECTING

—

Ronald de Leeuw, Director of the Van Gogh Museum, lives in a 17th-century house. On the ground floor, the bedroom and kitchen give on to a little garden of clipped box designed by the landscape gardener Michael van Gessel (above).

On the first floor, in the reception rooms, exceptionally fine Dutch 18th-century furniture mingles with objects brought back by Ronald de Leeuw from his travels. In his library, the complete works of Byron rub shoulders with those of Vondel, and set on a table are boxes disguised as books displaying casts of engraved gems of mythological subjects (opposite).

weekends listening to music and leafing through magazines and newspapers. As for the kitchen, it is a perfect example of the Dutch way of life in its refined simplicity. On the first floor the superb eighteenth-century Dutch furniture holds a silent and elegant conversation with souvenirs of Asian travels: nineteenth-century Japanese bowls and a gilded lacquer service made at the beginning of this century for a Netherlands ambassador to Tokyo. The master of the house receives visitors in his library on the same floor, where among ancient obelisks, plaster medallions and seventeenth-century paintings, pride of place goes to his first acquisition, a magnificent canvas of a *Gentleman with a Sunflower* (an intriguing anticipation for the young student who was to become the Director of the Van Gogh Museum when barely thirty-six years old) attributed to Gerard van Honthorst.

The same love of books – one of those great passions, like tobacco, coffee, and spices, that bind the people of Amsterdam together – appears in the writer and television person Boudewijn Büch. He has brought together the works of Goethe as well as a multitude of books about the poet, old atlases, Blaeu maps, travel books and anything about the dodo, the legendary extinct bird of Mauritius, in his immense library. It is built on two storeys, in exotic woods, with a gallery where a terrestrial globe has replaced the chandelier. It shows the familiar liking for comfort: the reader can choose to consult any of these bibliophilic marvels on a huge round table, or to sit and daydream pleasantly in the sitting area with its nineteenth-century furniture.

Strolling along the Prinsengracht, the walker may meet a man with a splendid red moustache.

In his wonderful kitchen, built to the same plan as that of the Bartolotti House so as to resemble the superb Dutch kitchens of the Golden Age, and furnished with simple country table and chairs (right), Ronald de Leeuw has had the table laid with Ginori Italian china and Dutch and French 18th-century glass and silver. Little Viennese covered bowls are set on the plates (above).

Boudewijn Büch, man of letters
and of television, takes refuge in
his library to seek inspiration
among the books he loves.
Designed by Pieter van der Zwan
and painted a very special shade of
blue copied from the 18th-century
Bibliotheca Thysiana in Leiden, it
is furnished with Empire pieces.
The 19th-century German papier-
maché globe has acquired a
splendid patina over the years
(left).

Couzijn Simon has composed a
strange ballet of dolls and antique
toys among the fittings of a former
Prinsengracht chemist's shop.
Rather incongruously in this very
18th-century décor, a painting by
Anton Heijbour reminds us that
Couzijn Simon is the exclusive
dealer in works by that artist
(above and right).

On the sitting-room walls Couzijn Simon has hung a collection of naïve pastel paintings and miniatures of the 18th and 19th centuries (left).

Above the original 18th-century chimneypiece of the red and green sitting-room, a Viennese toleware parrot seems to be looking at the same distant object as the pheasant painted on the overmantel (top).

All over the house, Couzijn Simon has arranged collections of coffee-pots, tin toys and anything connected with the world of childhood (above).

This is no ogre, even though he does look as if he has escaped from a fairy-story; it is Couzijn Simon who keeps shop in an eighteenth-century pharmacy that still has its original woodwork. There he sells old playthings, wax dolls and tin toys. The decorative scheme of his flat is as colourful as his moustache, which he dyes every Sunday. There is one pink and blue sitting-room crammed with naïve miniatures in pastels, and its counterpart in red and green, dominated by a wide Empire fireplace and peopled by a strange folk of wax dolls in languid attitudes from Hoorn (seventeenth century) or North Holland (eighteenth century), along with aeroplane-shaped biscuit tins and mechanical chickens and ducks which launch into an infernal saraband, beneath a beautiful eighteenth-century Dutch chandelier, when the clock strikes midnight. But in this rather unusual décor with its doll's-house charm, other surprises are in wait for the visitor, who will certainly not expect to find, on opening a door, an austerely tranquil sitting-room where modernity manifests itself in reproductions of chairs and tables in glass and chrome by Eileen Gray. Couzijn Simon, a whimsical character who seems to belong more to the world of Lewis Carroll than to the dull everyday world, also loves flowers, and in his enchanting garden (where a little pavilion houses the works of his painter friend Anton Heijboer, for whom he is the exclusive dealer) he grows gorgeous camellias in pots, completing the captivation of his visitors by the sheer fascination of a wonderful, secret, fragile world.

Another house, another world – but equally fantastic – with Peter Gabriëlse, where decadence and classicism rub shoulders, re-creating a world of ambiguity combining total realism with hallucination. In each of the models he has constructed from junk, looking like dolls' houses and inspired by eighteenth- or early nineteenth-century buildings, one object is shown quite out of proportion, focusing attention on its environment and puzzling the spectator like an unexplained allegory, giving him the sensation of being able to grasp the ineffable in an atmosphere of highly intriguing mystery.

The house is hidden away behind pleached limes beside a tributary of the Vecht. Everything in this late-nineteenth-century cheesemaker's farmhouse seems to be scattered around haphazardly, but after a while it becomes clear that the apparent disorder is the result of careful thought. Nothing in the choice or the arrangement of the objects is meaningless, and though they may look ordinary they are given significance by their role in a kind of dialogue. The show is everywhere, but it is discreet, allusive and adapts itself to the mood of the visitor, who is free to make what he will of these still lifes in the form of conversation pieces.

Remnants of a past that is touching in its humbleness survive in this décor of fantasy, such as the peasant's box bed of light-coloured wood left unvarnished and delicately carved, or the piece of furniture once used for storing peat, the principal fuel of a country poor in natural resources. In the sitting-room, panelled with plain wood, a Dutch desk and a cupboard full of Delft pottery re-create the timeless universe which the art-lover will irresistibly associate with traditional interiors containing plain, shapely objects carefully arranged so as not to force themselves on the spectator's attention, yet giving him something to think about. Those painted interiors, rather bare yet not unfriendly, always seem to conceal some mystery behind their commonplace appearance. Shut in on themselves yet wide open to view, they are like the narrative of a peaceful life, far from the

Peter Gabriëlse's studio and house seem to carry the beige and grey ghosts of his creations into everyday life. The fireplace in the sitting-room is ornamented with blue Delftware plates in a design derived from Chinese porcelain and with flaming torches carved in wood (below). Old books are stacked up in front of 18th-century shutters that were rescued from the scrap-heap (bottom).

In the calculated disorder of the studio, the odd collection of assorted objects will be assembled by the hand of the master to create a new work of art (right).

The 18th-century pastels hanging
in the studio of Peter Gabriëlse
are signed Jelgerhuis, an early-
19th-century itinerant painter who
travelled from town to town across
The Netherlands painting
portraits of the citizens. On the
1920s shop counter, a statue of St
Michael slaying the dragon stands
on a little watchmaker's cabinet
(above).

An 18th-century Dutch chair-
back stands against a panel of
Cordovan leather. These embossed
leather wall-hangings were
common to all 17th-century
patrician mansions. They were
painted with yellow varnish, using
a technique imported from Spain,
to give them a golden tone (left).

In the sitting-room, original
panelling frames two glass-fronted
cases stacked with Delft and Leeds
pottery (opposite).

dramas that trouble the outside world. Life is present, but cocooned. In the studio, a shop counter filling a whole wall brings together all the elements of this building, so harmonious in its restraint. The harmonies are subtle: Cordovan leather, ancient musical scores, mellow panelling, yellowed parchment. Peter Gabriëlse was born into a family of antique dealers. Old furniture, ornamental objects, utensils rescued from obsolescence – these were his childhood companions.

Perhaps Elsbeth van Tets's twins – model little girls – will recall their childhood with an antique-dealer mother in the same way, growing up in one of the most beautiful houses on the Keizersgracht that was built in the middle of the Golden Age and refurbished in the eighteenth century. This house, which serves as both family home and showrooms, seems to ignore the limits imposed by ordinary life and you are never quite sure where you are because the space reserved for clients feels so private. Going up a little staircase you come into a bedroom looking out over a very architectural 'Italian' garden. Higher up again is a sitting-room where Elsbeth van Tets, who can switch her attention effortlessly from chiné articles to masterpieces of Dutch painting (she is on the executive committee of the Mauritshuis in The Hague), collects objects acquired during her numerous trips abroad. In the semi-basement a kitchen, meticulously restored in line with seventeenth-century models, extends quite naturally into the garden, once again recalling the many paintings in which the artist offers the eye an escape route through a door left half-open to a courtyard or garden, creating an interplay between indoor and outdoor space: another example of the deep-rooted native tendency to openness.

On Elsbeth van Tets's staircase, a 'dummy board' (a wooden cut-out figure) contemplates an antique birdcage (top).

In the kitchen, under a hunting scene signed by the 19th-century Dutch painter John Hulk, are three quaint little chairs painted with stencilled designs from Stap Horst, a village near Zwolle (above).

The child depicted in a 19th-century English painting seems to be calling out to the three German dolls of the same period perched on a Victorian settee (opposite).

Twice a year Elsbeth van Tets, like her fellow proprietors in the neighbourhood, opens her house to the public. For the rest of the year she only receives by appointment and her visitors have the impression of being welcomed into a private home where business is not a matter of prime concern. In this she is like Anne-Paul Brinkman, a little farther down the Keizersgracht, an interior decorator and antique dealer who has amassed for his own pleasure a collection of furniture and *objets d'art* of extremely fine quality. He likes people to entrust him with the keys to their house so that he can get a feeling of the whole place, from the principal rooms to the smallest details, which often give the surest indication of a decided personal taste. Bringing to the twentieth century a baroque temperament inherited from the Golden Age, he likes to liven up a decorative scheme that may lack animation by introducing the unexpected. By playing with decorative elements of incongruous proportions he can organize an interior so as to give it breadth and intriguing perspectives.

The painter Corstiaan de Vries lives in a far more orderly environment of white and gold panelling that retires discreetly into the background, setting off the varied forms of his collection of old ivories as well as protecting them. It shows a surprising restraint on the part of this artist, by preference a portrait-painter, who lives in an early twentieth-century house, formerly the offices of a tea and coffee company, in the oldest part of Amsterdam. No such restraint appears in the rich collection of objects picked up on his frequent trips abroad and jumbled together in the most unexpected relationships. A vast bathtub sits under the questioning, meditative gaze of a large Tibetan Buddha, next to the table where the artist's friends gather

The romantic bedroom looks down on a little 'Italian' garden (above right).

The twins' attic room is furnished with two big 19th-century Dutch beds (right).

The centrepiece of Elsbeth van Tets's bright sitting-room, an animal painting by the early 18th-century Dutch artist John Griffier, hangs over an Empire banquette flanked by two small Italian hazelwood neo-classical commodes (opposite).

The 18th-century tiles set on either side of the cooking-hobs are decorated with little bird-cages, a typical motif of the period (left).

for impromptu dinner-parties, often accompanied by Beethoven sonatas played on an immaculate Bechstein grand.

Defying classification, these varied collections glimpsed in the course of personal contacts have in many cases been made for aesthetic reasons by people whose sole object was to create an arrangement of beautiful objects based on a deliberately subjective approach and ignoring all considerations of value, taking intrinsic beauty as its only criterion and distancing itself from prosaic collecting and financial speculation. Ever since the Golden Age Amsterdammers have enjoyed acquiring things, often spending fortunes on them, and although prodigality has no place in contemporary moral values, this passion – even sometimes tipping over into fantasy – has survived.

Anne-Paul Brinkman is both interior decorator and antique dealer and has just finished a complete conversion of his own house on the Keizersgracht where, surrounded by fine furniture and *objets d'art*, he greets customers and friends in a first-floor sitting-room. A 1920 self-portrait in mandarin costume by the Berlin painter Karl Homburg hangs above a Chippendale armchair upholstered in bright yellow standing on a parquet floor salvaged from a mansion in the Belgian Ardennes (right).

A traditional painted wooden bench stands in the entrance hall of the house where the portrait-painter Corstiaan de Vries lives. Sometimes these benches were carved with the owner's coat-of-arms (opposite).

Corstiaan de Vries has created a tasteful apartment in the former offices of a tea and coffee company. It is decorated with objects chosen for their appeal, symbolism and sense of humour. He composes them into careful arrangements, such as the 19th-century English manikin wearing a Florentine mask with an ivory rosary round its neck, set between two candle sconces of the same period on a mantelshelf discovered in a junk shop (above).

Cupboards have been built into the sitting-room panelling to contain an exceptional collection of ivories. The Italian lamps stand on a glass table-top supported by two elephants from Thailand (right).

In the entrance hall, lit by Louis XVI candelabra, an early-18th-century Dutch oval relief hangs above a collection of antique decanters of various origins (above).

For a few friends invited to supper, Corstiaan de Vries has arranged his table round a big bunch of Dutch tulips and set the yellow plates on solid silver platters with silver and silver-gilt cutlery and 18th-century glasses (left).

Amsterdam, richly decked as it is in the trappings of its Golden Age, is still mindful of the humbler aspects of its past. Down narrow streets of timeless calm, far from the throbbing life of its great canals, in a maze of blind alleys and tiny courtyards between churches and convents, countless small houses have for centuries watched over a simple way of life punctuated, in most cases, only by the comings and goings of seamen in the days when Amsterdam was still a great fishing port.

In the old port area an eminent cancer specialist lives in one of these little narrow-fronted houses, traditionally the homes of naval officers and revealing in certain significant respects how prosperous these people were, even among the working classes, in comparison with the rest of Europe. A floor paved in black and white marble, a Frisian cupboard, a little wooden chair painted by the craftsmen of Zaandam, a fountain set into the wall, fed by a rainwater tank – everything here fits into the picture of the old seafarers' simple way of life. Above the kitchen door a fat black cat purrs on the sill of an unexpected window: that of the garret where the maid used to live, always at hand and ready to come running when she was called.

Inez Stodel, who runs an antique shop in the Nieuwe Spiegelstraat (New Mirror Street), lives nearby in a small seventeenth-century house restored from top to bottom a dozen years ago by the previous owner, the architect Aldo van Eyck. It must be admitted that this street is not quite like others, since it originally comprised stabling rather than houses, which in many cases provided rear access to the great mansions of the Keizersgracht and the Prinsengracht (the little summerhouse at the bottom of the garden of the

SMALL HOUSES

—

This little street close to the harbour, a few yards from Admiral de Ruyter's house, was reserved for naval officers in the 18th century but nowadays attracts musicians, actors and doctors (above).

An eminent surgeon, his wife and daughter occupy an amazingly unspoilt period house. He sculpts, she plays the cello, and the little girl, who began learning the violin at the age of five, has left the half-size instrument made for her by one of her father's friends, and with her own head carved on the scroll, on a chair in the sitting-room. Bobby the farm dog has settled himself comfortably beneath the marble fountain built into the wall, which is fed from a rain-water tank (opposite).

Van Loon house is a perfect example of this). In one of the sitting-rooms a strongly geometrical chimneypiece is a lingering reminder of the last occupant. Inez Stodel has surrounded it with Dutch provincial furniture and some similar English pieces in the plain style that appeals to her, together with a collection of old jugs and examples of fine craftsmanship. However, the oddest piece of furniture in the house is undoubtedly a *Rippenvleugel*, a sort of baby grand piano invented in the 1930s for very small rooms. Its attraction, which can hardly reside in its beauty, is perhaps due to its oddity. In any case it did not appeal to music-lovers and the object, although intended for the mass market, is in fact a great rarity.

Ineke Schierenberg is an interior decorator as well as an antique dealer. She and her husband Dieter, one of Amsterdam's biggest antiquarian booksellers, specializing in natural sciences, live on one of the secondary canals in the centre of the city in a small house built in 1672 and hardly changed since then. The intimate scale of the rooms, the sitting-room with its walls covered in prints and furnished with Empire chairs, brightened by the vivid colours of some kilims and Kashmir textiles, all combine to create an atmosphere of tasteful warmth in a home where period details have survived into the present rather better than they have elsewhere. Take, for instance, the plasterwork drapery over the staircase, or the kitchen divided off from the sitting-room by nineteenth-century German bookshelves: the picture of serene, traditional domestic comfort.

Maryan Geluk, a determinedly conceptual artist, has settled in a *hofje*. Faithful to the principle of economy that characterizes her art, she has very

The antique dealer Inez Stodel
has made herself a very austere
environment. The centrepiece of
the room is a *Rippenvleugel*, a
strange kind of grand piano of the
thirties, standing on a painted
wooden floor (right). The rest of
the sitting-room decoration
consists of a lithograph of Java
and Sumatra, an English folding
governess chair, an African
stool and a Dutch Louis XVI
banquette. The two windows open
on to the garden designed by the
illustrious former occupant of the
house, the architect Aldo van
Eyck (above).

A painting done in 1860 by Albert
Raoux hangs above an English
provincial table on
which stand miniature pieces of
furniture, a collection of small
Dutch and Art Deco decanters
and a very rare 18th-century red
gin glass (opposite).

The conceptual artist Maryan Geluk lives in an unusual little house which looks out over Grill's *hofje*, eight little houses built in 1721 to form one of those rare and delightful little courtyards of almshouses. She has furnished her home with modern objects with uncluttered lines (right). A Rob Eckhardt lamp shines beside a Lae Molen lithograph and a sewing-machine base with a marble top (above).

Ineke Schierenberg, who specializes in the restoration of old houses, is not only an antique dealer but also does interior design.

In the charming little canal-side house where she and her husband live, she has been able to put her original ideas into practice. Behind the turn-of-the-century Berlin display cabinets which divide the sitting-room from the kitchen area, she has fixed a typical *damspiegel* (a pier-glass which served to enlarge the narrow rooms of this kind of house) between the windows, which are hung with 17th-century material (opposite).

little furniture – a reclining chair by the designer Rob Eckhardt, an armchair by Rijs Bakker – and some paintings on panel by Ronald Medema. From the windows she looks out on respectable old ladies tending their lawns and flowers in a peaceful atmosphere which the twentieth century seems to have completely passed by.

Time also seems to have overlooked the district round the Spaarndammerdijk (the Spaarndam Dyke) at the city limit on the Haarlem road, whose name commemorates one phase in the endless war waged by the Dutch against the North Sea. A few houses, suffocated by the city's rapid growth, huddle close around the church. Nearby, the painter Ger Lataster and his wife Hermine have moved into a house built in 1780. On the light wood floor of the white-walled sitting-room stands a Pleyel piano, testifying to the many-sided talents of the master of the house. Everything in this luminous world surrounded by its enchanting garden seems dedicated to protecting the artist in his retreat.

Crossing a romantic cemetery with tombstones standing among rampant weeds, you come to the house of the painter Ger Lataster, the former parsonage of a lovely old church. The windows of the huge sitting-room, whose wooden floor was salvaged from a warehouse, look out on a garden lovingly tended by Hermine, the lady of the house (above and below).

On either side of the door are large abstract expressionist pictures painted in emphatic brush-strokes by this artist, whose works include the ceiling of the Mauritshuis in The Hague (right).

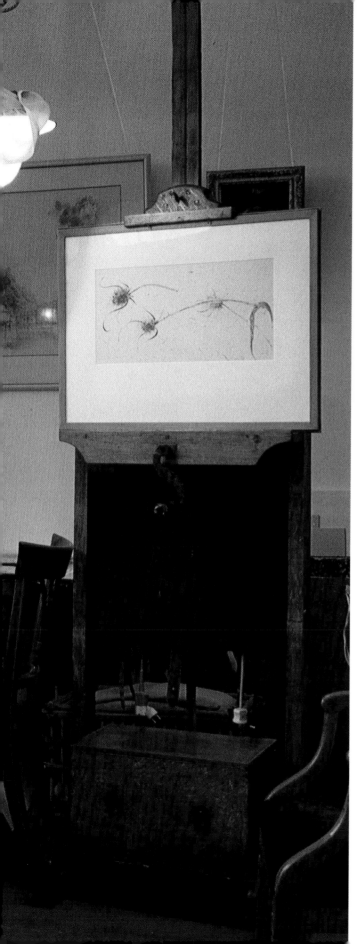

Portraits signed Willem Gerard
Hofker (her husband) and Georg
Rueter (her father), traditional
family furniture, objects brought
back from distant voyages: Maria
Hofker's flat sums up a life
dedicated to gardens, tradition
and travel. Some forty bound
volumes in a bookcase in her little
sitting-room contain exquisite
watercolours, poems and personal
reflections noted in finely penned
calligraphy. These are the fruit of
a long love affair between Maria
Hofker and her garden. Scattered
throughout the flat, watercolour
sketches and the full-blown roses
which she brings home every day
tell of her life-long passion.

At the heart of a very ordinary building in the
southern quarter of Amsterdam, the poetic world
created by Maria Hofker is hidden away in tiny
rooms cluttered with drawing-boards. Every day
she returns from her garden on the outskirts of
the city bringing drawings, watercolours and
notes which she works on during the winter days.
Dozens of bound volumes preserve a colourful
and fascinating record of these memories of her
garden. One of these precious originals is now in
the Rijksmuseum, but the curious can catch
some glimpses of this magical place by reading a
book she published a few years ago, *The Magic
World of Maria Hofker*.

Right in the middle of the old city, next to the
charming Oudemanhuispoort (Gate of the Old
Men's Almshouse), a passage lined with second-
hand bookstalls which runs through the University of Amsterdam, the writer and journalist Max
van Rooy lives in a narrow four-storey house
whose depth is far greater than its width,
combining a *voorhuis* and an *achterhuis* (front
house and rear house). Curiously, it has a
symmetrical façade with the entrance in the
centre, which is very unusual in the city. Here is
an intimate setting beside a public space where
books play an important part.

In the middle of a small peaceful street between the Herengracht and the Singel, not far from the Jordaan, a doorway, as is very common here, bears the name of its owner: Nooteboom. Between his frequent trips abroad, the writer comes back here to his books which overflow the shelves in every room, piled up on tables and desks but all arranged in perfect order. The front gable bears the date 1730, but the house is probably older than that. Its different levels, linked by those steep stairs that are so typical of Amsterdam's houses, offer a choice of delightful rooms according to the time and occupation of the day. Formerly inhabited by several families each crowded on to one floor (a herring seller occupied the cellar and a woman of easy virtue the attic), such houses have become fashionable as the workshops and small factories have moved away from the town centre, thus giving the area a more residential character.

It is the ease of transition between the entrance hall, with its great restraint, the intermediate floor and the basement that is most characteristic of Max van Rooy's house. The intermediate level, with its grey floor-tiles and high ceiling decorated with baroque mouldings, is dominated by a huge bookcase and a small collection of tubular furniture from among the classics of modern design (Mies van der Rohe, Le Corbusier and W.H. Gispen), while an elegant Empire banquette adorns the entrance (right). Every age produces its own remarkable works, and such pieces of exceptional quality go together and complement each other perfectly, as this house demonstrates.

The writer Cees Nooteboom, who lives between Majorca, Berlin and New York, has made Amsterdam his base for the past twenty years and is always happy to come home. He lives in a little house right in the historic centre. In his ground-floor sitting-room the *Encyclopaedia Britannica* is lined up beneath two 19th-century copies of Stations of the Cross painted in the Florentine style (opposite).

No electric wires or television aerials spoil the wonderful harmony of Holland's little villages. Pretty houses line the streets, each set in a flowery garden and freshly painted – grey in Broek in Waterland or green in Zaanse Schans (below).

On the Kadoelenweg, not far from the centre of Amsterdam, a small wooden house has been made into a museum. The owner has surrounded herself with examples of popular crafts, like these splendid enamelled buckets and cans, which have all been made locally in the Zaan and Waterland regions (above left and far right).

utc history consists of a series of glorious or dramatic episodes in which the sea is the heroine. Nowhere else has a nation captured its land from the water as it has here. Today, more than a quarter of its territory is situated below sea-level and has therefore been not only won from the waves but held against their continuous assault. As time goes by, further plans are developed and several thousand hectares of new polders are projected. The Dutch may have finished with conquering oceans, but they still yearn for the open sea. This maritime nation hangs its houses on the very edge of the windswept North Sea, and happily converts boats and barges into permanent homes on rivers and canals.

These extraordinary people have, by sheer force of will, succeeded in realizing dreams that must go back to their childhood. Thus you can still see, moored by the banks of the pretty Vecht, the *Zwerver* (Vagabond). This masterpiece in the Dutch tradition was the sublime, delirious brainchild of a visionary, the architect Wijnand Nieuwenkamp. Begun in 1898 and completed in 1902, it is a strange hybrid between a ship and a pot-bellied house-boat, concealing a very proper bourgeois interior with Delft tiles, solid wooden furniture, monumental chimneypiece and carved woodwork, spiced with a few exotic articles brought back from his many visits to Bali by Nieuwenkamp.

At the end of the last century house-boats did not exist and the idea of them, which seems so natural to us in this age of leisure activities, required a truly original mind. They often show a refined decorative style worthy of a good town house, and they can be perfectly restored since the tradition of fine craftsmanship has always been kept up.

LIVING ON
THE WATER

—

This extraordinary boat is moored beside the River Vecht opposite the village of Loenen (above). Designed and built at the turn of the century by W.O.J. Nieuwenkamp, a visionary architect who was determined to live on the water, the *Zwerver* is the oldest and most surprising house-boat in The Netherlands. When in 1902, after many difficulties, his dream had at last become reality, Nieuwenkamp and his wife moved aboard. Their initials and the date of their marriage are carved into the woodwork. This great traveller had spent a long time in Bali, from where he brought back objects and ideas which are incorporated in the boat's decorations (opposite).

By 1900 the steel hull, still a rather revolutionary idea, was finished. Then it was time to tackle the interior decoration. Nieuwenkamp turned to well-known cabinetmakers, who created a wonderful, warm interior in oriental teak, Lebanese olive-wood and Oregon pine, neglecting no detail in the search for total perfection. He had himself been an excellent wood-carver and examples of his own talented contribution are very much in evidence.

The moment Marinus Brandt set foot on the abandoned, derelict *Zwerver* in 1966 he fell in love with it. The boat, the first house-boat ever built in Holland, was for sale. This toy manufacturer with a passion for sailing bought it less than half an hour before an auction sale which might have brought ruin to its integrity. Restoration took several years, and nowadays his guests soon forget that they are on a boat, the traditional cosy atmosphere of Dutch houses having been so well adapted to a more confined space. Brandt, a perfectionist, was determined to restore the 'Vagabond' to its original appearance, using the notes that had survived in Nieuwenkamp's journal, but with modifications to suit his own taste. Now this historic vessel, moored in the widest part of the Vecht opposite the village of Loenen, has at last been restored to its original splendour.

House-boats have become numerous in the past few decades and some are wonderfully fitted out. One such belongs to 'Oom Willem' (Uncle William), a hero of children's television, who lives on a tributary of the Amstel near the exquisite village of Ouderkerk aan de Amstel in a setting worthy of Peter Pan. With only his sister's help, Edwin Rutten (his real name) completely restored his floating home in a month and a half, although the twelve-year-old vessel was

The vast, comfortable sitting-room of the *Zwerver*, with its Delft-tiled fireplace and traditional furniture, would not look out of place in a patrician mansion. Only when the chandelier swings do you remember you are on the water (opposite).

The television star Edwin Rutten, 'Uncle William' to adoring children, decided to live in a house-boat which he has furnished like a comfortable country house. He has always lived on the water, first in the centre of Amsterdam on the Prinsengracht, and now in the middle of the countryside on a tributary of the Vecht. In the dining-room, heated by a wood stove, a handsome window-frame converted into a mirror covers a whole wall and reflects the sitting-room. The round table topped with imitation marble standing on coconut matting has seen many candlelit dinners (above and left).

in an absolutely ruinous state. Cutting new
windows, arranging new bathrooms, installing
running water, telephone and fax, he made such
improvements that now nothing seems to be
lacking in this very English-feeling cottage concealed inside a rather modern hull. After the
excitement of a day spent in the television studio,
Edwin Rutten comes back to an almost childish
world. In the late afternoon he can always tell
the time by the neighbours who, whatever the
weather, plunge into the water punctually at six
o'clock for their daily half-hour dip.

For Aletta Moerman and her husband Robin life
on the water means sailing, not staying in one
place. They have taken up residence on the
Broedertrouw (Brotherly Love), a luxurious *tjalk*
(traditional Dutch sailing-barge) built in 1905.
Before becoming a pleasure-boat the *Broedertrouw* worked for many years transporting vege-
tables and agricultural produce on the Zuiderzee,

Among the lovers of life on the
water, the energetic remain at
their moorings during the week
and sail at week-ends. Aletta
Moerman and her husband Robin
live on a splendid *tjalk* built in
the early 1900s, very pleasantly
fitted out with light-coloured wood
and with a galley of comfortable
proportions (above and right). In
the cabin, where the dog Bobo
likes to stretch out, there is plenty
of storage space in addition to
cupboards of carved wood (left).
Moored during the week at one
of the prettiest quays on
Prinseneiland, they spend their
weekends all year round sailing
on the IJsselmeer and relaxing
in Holland's loveliest ports.
They enjoy competitions and take
part every year in the big Muiden
regattas which are held on the first
weekend in April and the last in
October, where a veritable fleet of
traditional flat-bottomed boats
gathers – *bolle schips*, *klippers*,
kotters and other *schuitjes*.

138

There is a severe housing crisis in Amsterdam and more than 3,000 house-boats and other vessels, side by side on the canals, relieve the pressure on overcrowded dwellings. Some are elegant floating houses with all possible conveniences – running water, electricity, window-boxes, little gardens, letter-boxes. Others, in a ruinous state, seem about to sink at any moment. It is impossible not to see, in the course of a boat trip on the canals, something of this life on the edge, which seems to be just as well ordered as everything else in Holland.

Edgar Parser, who is part Dutch and part English, is clearly crazy about sailing. He and his American wife Lyn have always owned a boat. They searched all the boatyards of Holland and France until at last, in the little port of Ghent, they discovered the *Westport*, the long Belgian-built canal-boat which now carries them over all the waterways of Europe. They engaged a Belgian decorator, Christophe Decarpentrie, to refurbish it for them in a modern style. The Parsers, as hospitable as they are obsessed with the arts, often organize cultural gatherings on their boat.

and its rather heavy shape indicates both its function and the rough conditions it often had to face. Heavy and hard to manoeuvre, this venerable vessel can manage seven knots when steered by the expert hands of Aletta and Robin Moerman, with all sails set and a good stiff breeze.

Lined with polished light-coloured wood, the capacious holds of the boat enclose a vast square space that has been fitted out for comfort. When it is not sailing, the *Broedertrouw* stays at its moorings among other elderly sailing-boats on the shore of Prinseneiland (Princes' Island). Every week-end, winter and summer, they set sail for the often misty landscapes of the IJsselmeer, the former Zuiderzee.

Lyn and Edgar Parser use their boat, built in 1930, to sail down the finest canals and to attend the most important cultural events, according to the season and their mood. *Westport*, a long canal-boat built in Belgium, can take them as far as Paris in the autumn for the International Contemporary Art Fair, up the Rhine to see the Lorelei and admire the castles high up on the river-banks, across Holland in spring through the tulip-fields, and even to Avignon in summer for the Theatre Festival.

The *Westport*, which has its moorings at Zaandam, was completely restored in 1985 by the Belgian decorator Christophe Decarpentrie, who rearranged the interior to sleep six in comfort, in a very contemporary atmosphere which faithfully reflects the owners' taste. To match the proportions of the boat, the furniture, as a final touch of perfectionism, was made on a slightly smaller scale than normal.

Aboard a *Helderse vlet* (a flat-bottomed boat from Den Helder), its gunwales protected by fenders of plaited rope, you arrive at the most unexpected house in the Amsterdam area, at Vinkeveen – a gorgeous little wooden house smothered in wistaria, perched on a scrap of land in a labyrinth of watercourses. In this region of former peat-bogs the houses are surrounded by pools of water scattered with little islands and the only way to reach them is by boat.

Christiaan van de Graaf and Els Hillenius designed and built their house with their own hands after a visit to Vermont. Nothing is missing from this extraordinary little home, tiny but comfortable, with armchairs and sofas arranged in front of a wood fire in the sitting-room. Lunch is taken in a conservatory overgrown with luxuriant foliage. In fine weather they sit in the shady garden where a pair of doves nest. The table and sideboard groan beneath jars of cherries in brandy, pickled artichokes and a hundred other original concoctions, such as the brightly coloured mixture of green and yellow cucumbers and whole gherkins prepared by Christiaan in early summer. It takes very little time for Els Hillenius and Christiaan van de Graaf to reach the bridal shop they have opened in Haarlem, for which they are also busy making bouquets and floral decorations.

Christiaan van de Graaf and Els Hillenius live in a house surrounded by nature and water which is only accessible by boat (above and below left).

The glass panels of the conservatory can be opened out in very hot weather. On an Italian tiled floor, the legs of a bistro table support a slab of blue stone on which plants flourish in pots. In front of the conservatory, an Indian planter's chair stands ready for sun-bathers (right).

Some of the houses on water are windmills, like that of Niels Daan, a biologist specializing in the study of fish. It was built in 1671, some twelve miles from Amsterdam in the Kennemerland region to the west of Haarlem, and he has slowly and meticulously restored it during six years of hard work and research. Crossing a kitchen panelled with broad wooden planks painted several shades of blue, including the 'fly blue' (intended to repel insects) that is to be found in so many Dutch interiors, you come to the sitting-room with its bronze-green and mustard-yellow woodwork and traditional Dutch furniture, such as the box bed, and the collection of clay pipes from Gouda. Then you must climb the old miller's ladder to reach the room of the master of the house, a spartan chamber of dazzling white-ness dominated by a superb wooden beam. Here, every object is perfect in its simplicity, such as the pair of ice-skates which bring to mind winter scenes by Isaac van Ostade. The peaceful atmos-phere attracts and fascinates Niels's friends, who love coming here. They have therefore estab-lished a tradition that at Christmas each of them must write a new chapter of a collective book, where the only rule is that it must never come to an end – even a happy one.

Five windmills once stood beside this lake in Kennemerland, a region famous for its mills. Only one remains. Three were destroyed by fire and the fourth broken up and sold. Known as the Tweede Broekermolen (Second Marsh Mill), this one was saved thanks to the last miller, who managed to purchase it; but its sails have not turned since 1930. Finally resigned to selling it, the miller put an advertisement in the papers. That was how the biologist Niels Daan became the proud possessor of a ruined 300-year-old windmill which was to cost him six years of work and patience to bring back to its former glory. The result is spectacular.

In the sitting-room, Niels Daan has torn out linoleum and wallpaper to reveal the original panelling, which he has painted in bronze-green and mustard-yellow. The cupboard at the end conceals the old box bed. On the table are books on biology, some seashells, fossils, birds' skulls and lichens found on the beaches (above).

Under an army mosquito-net, the bedspread in the room reached via the miller's ladder was made by Niels Daan's mother. An old Singer sewing-machine, a stuffed pike and antique ice-skates hanging from a beam complete this bare white décor, in which books are kept in a traditional linen-press (opposite).

Much of the kitchen has been painted in the lovely 'fly blue' which is so appropriate to old houses (left).

It was in the seventeenth century that the notables and well-to-do traders of Amsterdam acquired the habit of building themselves summer residences on the banks of rivers. The most famous architects of the age designed these dwellings, which from the late seventeenth century were strongly influenced by the Palladian villas on the banks of the Brenta near Venice. They are built as rural retreats, with large doors and windows. Very often they face on to the river – the Amstel or the Vecht – both for ease of transport and for pleasure.

It was on the Vecht in fact that Jacob van Campen, the architect of the Stadhuis (now the Royal Palace), started in 1627 to build Huis ten Bosch (the House in the Wood), whose severe, classically Dutch façade with its triangular pediment above heavy pilasters was to become the model for many other buildings.

A fortification had been built on this spot as a defence against the Normans in the ninth century, probably because the Vecht, at a point level with Maarssen, flows in a loop which commands the whole length of its course. Until 1593 the property took up all the land along the river at Maarssen, but then Aart ten Grotenhuys and Cornelis van Heemskerck divided it into two. One part became Het Huis ten Bosch, the other kept its old name of Het Goed ten Bosch (The Estate in the Wood). Later the first part was again divided, notably to accommodate the building of the Luxemburg and Overkerck country houses.

Huis ten Bosch is built in the shape of a T, on two storeys. A rather severe front door opens on to a hall paved with black and white marble and lit by a huge seventeenth-century brass chandelier. The hall extends into a corridor leading to an octagonal tea-house added in the eighteenth

COUNTRY
HOUSES

—

Huis ten Bosch is a perfect classical house, completely symmetrical, with a central door flanked by four pilasters creating a beautifully balanced façade (above).

A hundred years after the main building, an octagonal tea-house typical of Daniel Marot's style was built on to it. Well-to-do middle-class ladies of the 18th-century were mad about these miniature architectural masterpieces in which they could show off their refinement by organizing elaborate tea ceremonies. This little summer retreat has been redecorated by Ineke Schierenberg, who has inserted panels of toile de Jouy in the wood panelling, following designs by Fragonard (opposite).

century, typical of the little buildings that were then so fashionable, where high society liked to meet to converse and take light meals with no servants present. A *hoekbuffet*, a small cupboard fitting into a corner of the room, with finely carved woodwork, is a reminder of that very Dutch fashion and now holds a lovely collection of Chinese porcelain and a small sink of blue Soignies stone where the mistress of the house washed the fragile Kang Xi cups herself. From the eighteenth century, tea-houses were built away from the main house, often by a river so as to be able to enjoy the benefit of the lively scene created by the passing boats while also taking advantage of the coolness of the park.

The ceilings of all the ground-floor rooms, signed Antonie Hendricks, depict a marvellous display of birds' plumage and rustic scenes.

The property, which escaped destruction at the beginning of the nineteenth century, was later divided into four and sold at auction. Privately owned until 1922, it later became the official seat of the mayor before being sold to its present owners, who engaged the decorator Ineke Schierenberg to restore it to something of its former splendour.

Arend Jan van der Horst was employed to re-create the garden in the new space available, which had lost as much in area as in coherence. Now the children have the run of an immense lawn in front of the house with yew hedges clipped in the form of a garland. An enormous beech tree shades the tea-house and a flowerbed planted with an assortment of herbaceous and wild plants – lady's mantle, bleeding heart, and many others. Invisible from the house, the swimming-pool was built on the far side of a rose-garden, not far from a pond with a pretty bridge from which you can see a whole underwater world surrounded by hedges and sweet-scented roses.

In the village of Broek in
Waterland, most of whose large
wooden houses are painted grey,
the former burgomaster's
residence dates from 1775. The
little entrance hall, decorated with
stuccowork symbolizing the four
seasons, contains a typical Dutch
bench of painted wood and a table
with an antique lace cloth. The
18th-century hand-basin was
discovered in The Hague.

This garden has so many different aspects that everyone can find a favourite spot and the members of this large family can enjoy a real feeling of home life.

The early twentieth-century architects also tried to integrate their buildings into a natural setting. The spectacular house built at Laren in 1911 by Karel P.C. de Bazel, one of the leaders of the Amsterdam School, is reminiscent in its very British style of architecture of the kind of cottage that can be found in Dorset. The present owners chose two talented Belgians to carry out their renovations. Jacques Wirtz, a garden designer known all over the world for his topiary work,

Not far from the village of Laren, this big thatched villa was built in the early 1900s by the architect K.P.C. de Bazel, who specialized in country houses and was strongly influenced by English architecture. It had been ravaged by fire and was in a terrible state when the present owners came across it (above).

In 1984, the inspired Belgian landscape gardener Jacques Wirtz surrounded it with a garden of yew hedges, clipped box and pools of water, all closely tied in with the architecture of the house (left).

The verandah is an extension of the hall, paved with 1920s tiles with a geometric black-and-white border. Flooded with sunlight, it is charmingly furnished with little tables with long white tablecloths and flower-upholstered seats (right).

The Belgian antique dealer Axel Vervoordt decorated the sitting-room with its peach-coloured walls. A spectacular still-life by the 17th-century painter Jurmaen van Streeck hangs above a Spanish chest on which two candles are protected by glass chimneys. The owners of the house, great lovers of old paintings, travel the length and breadth of Europe in search of works to add to their collection.

On an English Georgian table in the centre of the room stands a flower arrangement by their neighbour, the florist Marcel Wolterinck (above).

The garden, with its contrasting patterns of brick against grass, leafy arbour and pool, displays the virtuosity of Jacques Wirtz (left and opposite).

In Valérie's romantic bedroom, Ralph Lauren fabrics mix with Dutch peasant material found in the Albert Cuypstraat market in Amsterdam (above).

Many of the decorative objects in the house were found by the Antwerp antique dealer Axel Vervoordt, such as this 18th-century Italian statue (left).

Twenty years ago, the interior decorator Jan des Bouvrie found a gorgeous twenties house, complete with stabling for his horses, in the middle of the woods that cover the Bussum region. Nowadays his other activities have forced him to give up riding, but he still keeps six horses for the use of his friends (opposite).

In the lovely sunken garden dotted with statues and adorned with pretty little bridges he designed himself, two stone lions guard the steps to the lawn. The sundial set in the middle of a bed of lavender continues a very Dutch custom (above).

In 1990 Monique and Jan des Bouvrie added a verandah to the house to make it bigger. All in black and white, it is furnished with a little Eileen Gray table, Maroeska Metz jardinières, and armchairs designed by the owner (left).

was engaged for the park, while the Antwerp antiquarian Axel Vervoordt brought together an impressive collection of furniture, tastefully arranged and enhanced by an exquisite selection of exceptionally fine paintings, particularly of the seventeenth century, which the owners collect avidly. The most notable works are by Jan Brueghel the Elder, Judith Leyster and Jan Miense Molenaer. In this cosmopolitan setting, luxury and comfort flourish unrestrained, a rare feature in a country where restraint is the norm.

At first sight the house of the fashionable decorator Jan des Bouvrie at Bussum seems first cousin to the previous one, but as soon as you pass through the door you realize that you are in a very different world. The stables and their snorting occupants suggest a more countrified residence, but a well-ordered one, and the frankly contemporary taste of the master of the house is given full rein. He is a purist who will have nothing but the work of the greatest cabinet-makers or of famous painters and designers. The plainness of the ensemble is reduced to black and white in the beautiful conservatory built on to the house: the visitor is immediately conscious of being in the home of a professional.

Laren is a small residential town some twenty miles to the east of Amsterdam. In this heavily wooded area of Gooiland a number of very pleasant houses have been built to make a quiet retreat only half an hour away from the city centre. Ten minutes by bicycle from his flower-shop, Marcel Wolterinck, at thirty the most successful florist and landscape gardener in the country, has found a little house dating from the twenties. It is rather dark but has a most romantic atmosphere and he has made it his home where he welcomes both friends and

A jardinière by Maroeska Metz shows off its curves in front of the window (above).

Jan des Bouvrie was always full of creative ideas, even when he was a child. He has been known to redecorate his bedroom several times in one year. In the one where he and his wife sleep at present, and for which he has designed two white armchairs softly lit by Ingo Maurer lamps, only the fitted carpet brings a touch of colour. The painting of an unmade bed on the far wall is by a Dutch artist, Rob Rats (right).

clients. On the east front, at the back of the house, he has created a vast, high conservatory, paved with rough stone, which extends the sitting-room space, forming a link between house and garden. A floral arrangement sits on a large circular table, a little landscape in itself in the midst of a natural setting.

Outside the sitting-room windows the garden has kept its original character and nature seems to have taken over, though in fact it is fully under control. What look like wild flowers, growing in the woods round about, are sensitively nurtured here and seem to be mounting an invasion on the house, backed by a heavy mass of rhododendrons. The dining-room faces out to the north of the house on to two patios with ochre-coloured walls. On the first one, surrounded by clipped yews, a large wooden table designed by the owner is used for eating out in summer. The second patio is a shady garden decorated with clipped plane-trees.

A wonderful world hides within the brick walls of the small twenties house where Marcel Wolterinck, a thirty-year-old florist and interior decorator, lives with his family. Plants and objects are blended in a poetic harmony (above and below left).

In the yellow sitting-room, the two screens covered with sailcloth, like the sofa, are finished off with outsize bows. The chandelier, made to measure in Wolterinck's own shop, hangs over a table covered with an Indian cloth on which are set a selection of objects chosen for their visual appeal (right).

In the kitchen, which Marcel
Wolterinck has completely
remodelled to give it a provincial
look, are a rustic table and six
chairs picked up in France.
Attractive wicker hampers are
used as storage on the shelves
(above).

Wire stands, turned-ash
candlesticks, stone balusters and a
coronet of artificial flowers – a
series of such simple details adds
to the richness of this splendid
décor (right).

The master bedroom extends on to a huge terrace which juts out over the garden. On the wooden floor painted wine-red and edged with a broad band of black stand two easy chairs upholstered in toile de Jouy and a tester bed over which a mosquito-net is gracefully draped (above).

In a salute to the marble floor-tiles of the patrician mansions, the floor and the bath in the comfortable adjoining bathroom have been painted in black and white squares. A luxuriant fern thrives atop its column (left).

Georgette Reuchlin, an interior designer known for the warm and imaginative qualities of her work, lives at Bloemendaal (literally, Vale of Flowers), a residential district of Haarlem set in the midst of the Kennemerduinen national park, whose immense dunes shelter a great number of protected bird species. In a residential estate designed by the celebrated landscape architect Leonard Springer, her huge house, packed with treasures, opens on each side on to gardens of different colour schemes, while the trees have been left to grow on the hillsides and the lower part left as pasture where cows graze.

The white garden, visible from the sitting-room, is constructed round a circular pond fed by a stream. It is planted with *Schneewittchen* (Snow-white) roses, *Hosta crispula* (plantain lily) and *Alchemilla mollis* (lady's mantle). In spite of its limited dimensions, the garden is built in two terraces, which compensate for the unevenness of the terrain while also increasing the area exposed to the sun, which can thus be enjoyed until it sets.

The green garden, a wide lawn surrounded by trees and bushes, offers a pleasant extension to the sitting-room, while the dining-room gives on to a covered terrace, which stays deliciously cool for summer meals.

These *buitenhuizen* (outside houses) as such country properties used to be called, are in fact the setting for a very urban life-style. Refurbished with a profound feeling for comfort and with great care to preserve the beauty of the past, and at the same time asserting their individuality by a few anti-conformist but tasteful touches, they have all the irresistible charm that gives Amsterdam and its environs such appeal.

Pierre and Georgette Reuchlin live with their children in the pretty village of Bloemendaal in a house built in 1910 by the architect Baanders. When they found it, it was in a terrible state. Georgette, a talented interior designer, immediately saw its possibilities and decided to move there. She worked miracles. The verandah, which extends the house towards the lovely garden redesigned by Arendt Jan van der Horst, was built some ten years after the house (above).

In the small sitting-room, the chairs and sofa covered in Milanese silk and Indian Paisley shawl material come from Georgette Reuchlin's shop. An Empire desk and an 18th-century French console table complete the décor (right).

The master bedroom, decorated with English and French printed fabrics in harmonious shades of blue, has a particularly welcoming atmosphere. The decorator had the idea of adding pediments to the wardrobes and hanging a papier-mâché tray above the bathroom door (above).

In the dining-room, a set of Dutch Louis XVI chairs are covered with *trijp*, Utrecht velvet, which was used from the 17th century onwards, but which went out of fashion at the end of the 18th century and is now only made in one factory, at Hengelo (left).

The lovely early 20th-century architecture is complimented by the choice of warm colours, bright fabrics and antique furniture, in which the English influence favoured by the owners is very evident. In the staircase well an 18th-century portrait of an English member of the family and Colefax and Fowler curtains frame an English sofa (opposite).

Amsterdam has always asserted its freedom, both in the choices made and in the projects undertaken. Lacking the usual attributes of a capital city – no embassies, no ministries – it nonetheless enjoys all the status of a true capital. From Amsterdam with its privileged position has flowed a stream of new ideas that have spread all over the country and often beyond its frontiers. This city whose pattern of canals suggests introspection, which appears to be a cul-de-sac backed by an invisible sea, is in truth an inexhaustible source of experiments, of ventures into the unknown, of new theory and new practice.

Amsterdam, an eminently secular city, has manifested a taste for freedom all through its history. A tolerant city, proud and rich in its cosmopolitanism, it has welcomed the most innovative notions and protected their development, while always keeping at a certain distance as a way of allowing them wider freedom. Long after it had ceased to be Europe's favoured centre of commercial trading and exchange, Amsterdam retained and cherished its curiosity; its wealth often permitted dreams to become reality more easily here than elsewhere.

The Dutch are experimental magicians when it comes to conjuring up new kinds of accommodation. Whether in transforming the warehouses in the long-abandoned area of the former port, or those along the canals – whose façades can only be distinguished from those of dwelling-houses by their shutters – or in restoring deconsecrated churches for use as residences, as artists' studios or as galleries, everything in the way of attractive and efficient conversion is susceptible to their enterprising spirit.

The Amsterdammers, who are prepared to go to any lengths in order to continue living in a city which they love but which cannot be enlarged

CONVERTED SPACES

—

The Amsterdammers, enchanted by the idea of at last being able to live in large spaces, have converted all sorts of industrial buildings into dwellings, like this tobacco factory dating from the end of the last century. Special authorization was needed to build the little bridge across the canal to reach it (above).

This former clandestine church on the Singel, with nothing to show where its entrance is, is remarkable. The windows have retained their original shape. Walls painted several shades of grey, pale pine floors, furniture acquired from many sources and an abundance of green plants create a harmonious background to this tranquil world (opposite).

indefinitely, have often pioneered the invention of new areas of living space. This pragmatism probably springs from certain aspects of their moral attitudes – a spirit of tolerance, respect for the rights of others and openness being essential factors in launching such innovative experiments.

Wherever would this young woman have been able to find the three hundred square metres (about 3,200 square feet) she needed to live in, except in a church overlooking the Singel? The early seventeenth-century building, rich in history, was a brewery before being converted into a chapel by the Anabaptists. They modified its structure and built a central arcade, two apses, and a double gallery on the first floor carried on Doric columns. It returned to secular use, becoming an auction house until 1988. Its present owner, with help only from a builder and some friends, turned this magical but somewhat improbable setting into a dream house. Partitioning off only as much of the available space as was indispensable for functional requirements, she preserved its proportions and its original colour, making pale grey the basic shade in the decorative scheme. Here nothing could be kept to normal scale. The indoor plants are as big as trees, the oak benches are enormous and, by a stroke of luck, when another church was closed down she acquired some imposing altar candlesticks which look as if they had been here for ever.

The same sense of space, so rare in a city where the houses seem to jostle each other in the search for light, can be found in the Jordaan with its narrow streets lined with modest dwellings. Here the fashionable photographer Rollan Didier has converted an old grain warehouse, which for

Fascinated by violent colours, the fashionable French photographer Rollan Didier covered a set of imitation Louis XVI chairs, which he found in the Salvation Army shop, in multi-coloured satin (left).

In this old grain-store which had been turned into a children's cinema – a huge space of more than 500 square feet lit by a skylight in the roof – he built three oval structures which he calls his 'deserted towers' and which house the staircase, the kitchen and a multi-functional office mounted on castors. The chair by the Pleyel piano was designed by his friend Dicky Huese (right).

some time did duty as a cinema, into his home. Or you can find it on Prinseneiland, not far from the port, in the old Insulinde (East Indies) warehouse restored by the painter Ans Markus; or in the former warehouse now occupied by the sculptor Waldo Bien, which seems to rock like a boat when the wind blows.

At the home of Tom and Hoedel van Leeuwen – he is a teacher of architectural history, she has worked for many years at the Van Gogh Museum which she helped to create – their first concern was to save all they could of the former warehouse on the Herengracht which they had found in a dreadful state of disrepair. Here, blond wood forms a background for the brilliant colours of Turkish kilims, while Indonesian cinema posters and pictures painted in the style of Edward Hopper by Tom van Leeuwen create a decorative scheme which is more carefully thought out than may seem at first sight, and where intimacy is never driven out by conviviality.

Artists, always in search of light and space for their studios, are extremely alive to the advantages of disused warehouses. Ans Markus – an actress and painter whose magic-realist works are made up mainly of self-portraits and many portraits of the Dutch Royal Family – lives in one on Prinseneiland, one of the Westelijke Eilanden (Western

Islands), a sort of city archipelago where the merchants of the Golden Age used to store their goods and have their ships repaired. She has filled it with her work and furnished it with modern seating, like the Geoffrey Harcourt armchair which she found, along with the round dining-chairs, at Arti Fort.

Waldo Bien (right) has deliberately refused to make any improvements that would have spoiled the authenticity of his surroundings, and he has kept the rope and pulley (which are useful for bringing up shopping), the miller's ladder (which does for a staircase) and the windows (which open on to emptiness).

This vast space was once a sugar warehouse, then a barrel-organ restorer's workshop, before becoming the lair of this artist who takes enormous photographs in far-off lands and then repaints them as superb pictures.

Before they began the conversion of a 1718 silk warehouse, Tom and Hoedel van Leeuwen camped out there to get used to living with the very special light of the place. The spacious bedroom, looking out in two directions, is so bright that they sometimes spend the whole day there working, reading, watching films and listening to music by their favourite composer, Rossini (above left).

In the bathroom, in which the original double-lavatory arrangement was their own idea, the shower curtain is made from a flag which they brought back from Milwaukee (left).

All the photographs and original documents connected with the house are kept in a corner of the room, together with the book by Caspar Philips, who made drawings of all the houses along the Keizersgracht and the Herengracht between 1768 and 1771 (below).

When he is not deep in writing his architectural tetralogy, Tom van Leeuwen makes models or paints – as can be seen from the pictures which hang over the English marquetry desk with its lamp based on a design by Frank Lloyd Wright. Lunch can be taken in the sunlight looking out over the Herengracht from a little table by the window (opposite).

By contrast, at the house on the Keizersgracht of the Argentine painter Carlos Ré and the antique dealer Gerard Witlox, everything has been transformed into decoration. The floors are hidden under marble *trompe l'oeil*, the kitchen furniture is covered with drawings, the bathroom is a vast sampler of coloured tiles applied like mosaic over walls and floor, while terracotta busts, console tables, marble sculpture and English furniture crowd the interior with a kaleidoscope of colours and textures. One old lady can still remember this strange home some decades ago when it was the stable block of the Van Loon house. She is the daughter of the last coachman there and remembers the dressage sessions organized by Hendrick van Loon, who taught his horses and dogs to dance to the strains of an orchestra concealed in this very hayloft.

Diametrically opposed to this is the home of fashion journalist San Ming, who has created a very New York ambiance in his loft close to the Vondelpark, in the heart of a quiet, well-to-do district much favoured by professionals. In a 1921 building in the style of the Amsterdam School but with a degree of luxury uncommon to that style, orientated as it was towards municipal estates, he has used the space to create a white and pale-toned universe where the only touches of colour are the book-covers. The armchairs upholstered in white canvas, some articles of thirties furniture and some unusual objects found in junk shops or skips combine in a static decorative scheme in which each piece of furniture, each object, has found its ideal, immutable place.

Unlike San Ming, who moved away from the centre of Amsterdam in search of space, Margreet and Peter Beerents have managed to

Carlos Ré and Gerard Witlox have kept some of their rooms in a classical style, like the sitting-room with its neo-classical bookcase designed by Gerard Witlox (top). Other rooms, like the kitchen floored with sample tiles from a bankrupt factory, suggest a dizzy aestheticism (above).

Another sitting-room has a floor painted in *trompe-l'oeil* marble (right).

San Ming has treated his apartment in an Amsterdam School building like an American-style loft. He has rejected any intrusion of colour into the decoration and has introduced many subtle refinements, such as the white line edging the floors, the broad linen ribbons which hide the picture-hangers, and the Kraft paper on the walls. Beside the former serving-hatch converted into an aquarium, the blade of a sawfish stands beside a large American painting of the forties and a work by Jo Baur, a member of the 'Amsterdamse Joffers' group, which comprised a number of wives of Dutch painters in the fifties (left).

A painting by Teixera de Mattos hangs above a console table bearing two marble church candlesticks and an Amsterdam School newel-post ornament (above).

reconcile both requirements by refurbishing a former tobacco factory built in 1890 on the Oudezijds Voorburgwal, one of the most peaceful, charming canals in this very old part of the city. When they found this amazing building, its nicotine-yellowed walls exuding a persistent smell of tobacco, Margreet Beerents installed her fashion-design studio in a room which still contains its sample tables, looking like school desks. To enliven the space, which might easily have seemed excessively empty, she has created subtly organized groupings, often centred on one piece of furniture such as an old sideboard loaded with white and gold china or a long table covered with period linen with rattan armchairs drawn up around it. In the former boardroom the moulded ceilings, mellow panelling and Edwardian lamps create the melancholy, abandoned atmosphere of a deserted mansion. Peter and Margreet have made this their bedroom with its windows overlooking the canal that was nicknamed the *Fluwelenkanaal*, the Velvet Canal, when the rich burghers used to parade up and down it in their fine apparel made from that luxurious fabric.

Margreet and Peter Beerents have set themselves up in the premises of a late-19th-century tobacco factory. The showroom has become the workplace for Margreet, a fashion designer, where she receives her clients (right).

In the bedroom, the early 20th-century ceilings, panelling and lamps recall the time when the tobacco manufacturers held their meetings there. It is now decorated with all sorts of objects picked up by the owners on their travels – the pier-glass comes from Belgium, the two wooden bedside lamps from Italy, and the wicker chairs were unearthed in the Amsterdam flea-market (opposite).

The only buildings on Prinseneiland, a small island to the west of the harbour, were previously warehouses and shipbuilding yards. Nobody used to live there. Nowadays all the warehouses have been converted into residences and small shipyards keep up the tradition, restoring old boats or building new ones. One of these is overlooked by the windows of the huge grain warehouse that Yvonne Hulst recently moved into. Marianne van Brussel designed this new living-space in which its owner could give free rein to her taste for contemporary decoration principally inspired by the Italian version of post-modernism. Frankly admitting, like many other enlightened amateurs, her lack of faith in Dutch design, which so often is no more than an impersonal compromise between different tendencies derived from Paris or Milan, she allows very little room for the creations of her fellow-countrymen, with the exception of Rob Eckhardt, Borek Sipek and Maroeska Metz, a young woman who transforms iron into amazing lamps, candelabra and chandeliers.

In this former grain warehouse, Yvonne Hulst has rehabilitated the beams and reorganized the interior space. The harem couches were made to measure by Binnenhuis (opposite).

The small bedroom is lit by a Maroeska Metz candle-holder (left).

The tableware is by Borek Sipek, the Prague designer now established in Amsterdam (right).

These vast spaces reclaimed from former industrial buildings might seem frightening to those brought up to a world of narrow horizons, but they are ideal for people who are enchanted by the possibility of living without bumping up against walls on every side. Today, in Amsterdam as in other capitals, they have become obligatory symbols among certain professions for which the current fashion is everything.

Thus the decorator and furniture designer Dicky Huese has moved into a former ship chandlery dating back to 1640 close to the harbour. The basic idea was to paint all the walls in bold, unexpected colours. Using her own creations, she has made an original world: the feet of the chests of drawers recall the forms of Russian cathedrals, armchairs are disguised as storks, high-chairs look like funnels, tables are divided up like jigsaw-puzzles and screens are ghostly silhouettes. At the back of the house, a romantic little garden crowded with flowers and an incongruous hen-coop seems to be wondering what it is doing in such company. Moored at the base of the warehouse, a tug straight out of an animated cartoon awaits the sightseer who wants to explore the city by canal.

Dicky Huese is not only an interior decorator and producer of advertising films, but also designs her own line of furniture. She is photographed beside a painting by Zsoka Rektenvald, leaning against a 'Triangle Affair' chair, one of her own creations, as is the 'Black Tulip' lamp. Behind the 19th-century armchair covered in purple cloth she has arranged an amusing set of contemporary Italian glasses. The slender lines of a group of fifties vases on the window-sill are silhouetted against the light.

The architect Marianne van Brussel decided to remodel a magnificent apartment in a 1919 block built by F.A. Warners in the museum district. She has converted it with taste and intelligence, respecting the characteristics of the architectural style by giving them prominence. Freeing the volumes of the space, the furniture chosen by Yvonne Hulst fits naturally into place.

Henriette Daniels, who is a fashion designer, determined to favour the creative artists of her own country by choosing a young Amsterdam architect, Jeroen van Schooten. He has kept almost nothing but the façade of the large building she bought on the Keizersgracht. The

Dicky Huese has refurbished a 1640 ship-chandlery opposite the old port. The rails on which the little wagons ran that carried the goods are still there, integrated into the floor. The decoration with its splashes of wild colour shows a well-disciplined madness. In the dining alcove, the graphic lines of the table designed by her complement those of the glaring red carpet (above).

In the sitting area, a pedestal table painted by Paul de Lussenet holds the television set. A late-19th-century armchair and another found in the flea-market stand beside the low table made by the designer, lit by a Venetian glass lamp of the fifties (left).

Two architectural spirals balance each other on either side of the huge living space. One conceals the staircase with its old stone steps, the other hides the kitchen. The fifties armchairs have been re-covered in shocking purple velvet, giving them an air of film-star glamour (right).

The apartments built by the Amsterdam School have generous dimensions that make them extremely pleasant places to live in. This hall designed by the architect F.A. Warners has been refurbished by Binnenhuis (opposite).

Henriette Daniels's sitting-room with its four front windows and high ceilings is the perfect answer to her need for space. The sofas round the glass table match the strong colours of a Luigi Carboni painting and two Anatolian kilims, while a pair of armchairs by Eileen Gray complete the décor (above).

The painter Paul de Lussanet decided to install both his flat and his studio on the first floor of an old cosmetics factory. He chose bright colours to decorate the corridor leading to the studio (left).

interior of this 1939 office block had consisted of a succession of small unconnected rooms, some of them only accessible from outside. Henriette wanted light and space, so the architect restructured the whole building, creating new spaces and adding balconies overlooking the garden as well as spiral staircases. The owner looks on the decoration as a long-term project, taking her time to test the space and bring the new dimensions under control, moving a piece of furniture again and again until it finds its proper place.

Paul de Lussanet, quite the most Parisian of Amsterdam painters (he spent fifteen years by the banks of the Seine), cannot now imagine ever moving away from the canals of his native city. With a group of friends he bought a former cosmetics factory on the Prinsengracht. Keeping the workers' metal cupboards as well as the lift, he chose a futuristic decorative scheme by Dicky Huese for his office, while Karel Doorman designed him a couch and Rob Eckhardt an amazing leaning lamp.

But the wind of modernism does not only blow on warehouses and commercial buildings. Traditional houses along the canals have not been spared, and they conceal gems of creativity behind their classic façades. Barbara Farber has

Jules and Barbara Farber have created the feeling of a loft in a traditional 17th-century house by removing the dividing walls to make a bright, spacious sitting-room with its three windows looking out on the Keizersgracht. A painting by Ray Smith dominates the Italian armchairs and sofas (opposite).

The magnificent ceiling in the art gallery depicting King Solomon and the Queen of Sheba dates from 1735. The unknown artist appears to have been inspired by drawings made by Daniel Marot in 1712 (left).

made an apartment over her gallery of contemporary art, where the works are displayed in vast white rooms with spectacular eighteenth-century painted ceilings. On the private floor, contrasting with the white walls, a huge multicoloured palette painted by the Englishman Tony Cragg reminds us that artists are at home here. On the light-coloured parquet floor, Italian designer furniture rubs shoulders with work by the gallery's artists: cut-down objects by the Frenchman Bertrand Lavier, *Arte Povera* sculptures by Paolini, kitsch dancing-pumps by Rhonda Zwillinger of New York, and a startling composition of a cow lying on its side by the Englishman Bill Woodrow.

The spectacular rearrangement of this space within a traditional canal house was devised by Ed Veenendaal, who himself lives in another classic house built on the Amstel by Adriaan Dorsman. He has succeeded in creating a vast open-plan apartment on what used to be the reception level when a single owner occupied the whole house. There was therefore no bathroom or kitchen on this floor, and they have been ingeniously fitted in – the bathroom within the existing room and the kitchen in a former bookcase with brightly painted woodwork. With the walls removed, the new space is articulated round a hall which retains its original decoration by Gerard de Lairesse. Sumptuous plasterwork typical of the great merchants' houses, nineteenth-century parquet floors, Directoire glass-fronted cabinets and Napoleon III chandeliers mingle with the modern creations of Dicky Huese, of the painter Paul de Lussanet, the sculptor Alexander Schabracq and the Czech designer Borek Sipek, who lives and works in Amsterdam and whose neo-baroque creations are exhibited in the great museums.

The architect Ed Veenendaal and his antique-dealer wife Ingeborg live by the Amstel on the first floor of a spectacular house built by the architect Adriaan Dorsman. The union of their temperaments, combining respect for the old with a taste for the avant-garde, has produced a spectacular result. The very finest Dutch design is represented here.

In the pink bedroom, a number of charming objects are arranged on a Bulgarian marquetry secretaire to create a romantic effect (above).

Ed Veenendaal has placed some unusual items in the hall with its splendid stuccowork by Gerard de Lairesse – balcony columns, a painting by Duyfor, and, beyond the piano, a palm-tree which echoes the motifs in the plaster (right).

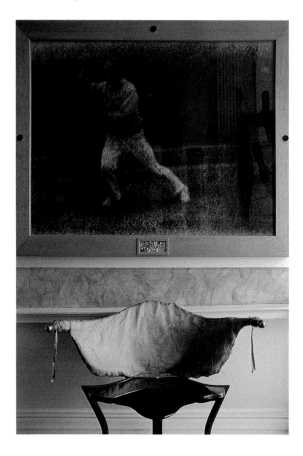

The 'Bambi' chair, one of Borek Sipek's best-known designs, stands under a painting by Christian Bastiaan (above).

Ed and Ingeborg Veenendaal have installed their kitchen in the former library and furnished it with a table and cupboards of lacquered wood designed by the architect. He has fitted a stove hood into the old fireplace and surrounded the table (laid with Spanish china) with curious Memphis chairs that have backs shaped like table-mats. In this hospitable room the Veenendaals regularly hold dinner-parties at which they serve traditional dishes like *hutspot*, hotchpotch (right).

Gardens and Flowers

In the land of the tulip,
where flowers are a national passion,
gardens are precious, intimate spaces
shielded from the clamour of the city.
Their straight lines match those of the
canals, forming a softer mirror-image of
the façades of the houses.
Where flowers take their place by every
stretch of water, the garden is as much
an object of meditation and reflection
as it is of pure pleasure.

By Arend Jan van der Horst

Straight lines impose on Dutch gardens a subtle order according to which all space, whatever its dimensions, is governed by perspective. The Dutch landscape is chequered with canals and watercourses which suggest a kind of abstract art that prefigures Mondrian's painting. Nothing here is wild; space has been conquered by force, preserved by science; nature is the result of artifice. In these vast landscapes where the horizon does not seem to exist except in the fringe of dunes on its maritime borders, earth and sky appear to meet. Everything is a matter of light, and the rest is left to man to organize.

Water is everywhere. Firmly held back above land level, entering and retreating with the tides, it irrigates the lung, or the heart, that governs life. Water is both a danger and a vital resource, it means both terror and energy. The Dutch garden, in its rigorously organized role of meeting the pressure exerted by this omnipresent factor, often seems to be a metaphysical reflection on nature rather than a simple object of pleasure.

Apart from its quays and some rather irregularly shaped parks created in the nineteenth century, Amsterdam appears to be a city in which nature is confined to the countless potted plants that the passer-by glimpses behind the tall glazed openings of the windows; but this would be a paradox in a nation where gardening has played such an important role for centuries. In reality, as in many other capital cities, nature is there, but it is hidden as if reserved for the somewhat selfish pleasure of a few privileged people. Behind the façades of the high houses along the canals there are often hidden gardens which, with space frugally limited, and in most cases allowed much greater depth than width, have endured the changes wrought by time with varying degrees of fortune. In some cases, the pavilions built at the

In the green countryside along the banks of the Vecht, rich merchants constructed sumptuous dwellings, some of whose tea-houses, in a variety of styles, have survived. One such is that of Loenersloot designed in the 17th century by the French architect Daniel Marot and meticulously restored (above). Others were of a more rustic nature (top). The one in the garden at Blijdenstein in the village of Nieuwersluis enhances the romantic aura of its setting (opposite).

bottom of the garden as tea-houses or to shelter plants or carriages have survived to become very agreeable and sought-after retreats, providing an escape from noise and bustle without leaving the heart of the city. These pavilions, which usually echo the design of the house front, give structure to the shape of the garden by providing an inorganic element. There are plenty of names to describe them: gloriettes, summerhouses, even simply arbours. Gloriettes belong essentially to town gardens. Some have been preserved, like the one in the Van Loon garden or that in the Prince Bernhard Foundation on the Herengracht which houses the Foundation for the Protection of Historic Gardens in The Netherlands.

Tea-houses appeared in the seventeenth and eighteenth centuries in the big properties built by wealthy merchants along the Vecht. These structures, very diverse in form and material with glass playing an important part, were often built beside the water, providing a pleasant setting in which to take tea while contemplating the comings and goings of boats on the river. Nowadays they are lovingly restored, often with the help of the Department of Historic Monuments, like the one at Loenersloot designed by Daniel Marot. Their number and their variety — from the bulb-shaped seventeenth-century roof to the nineteenth-century thatch — lend additional charm to a boat trip.

In contrast to English parks or French gardens, the Dutch dimension has always been one of restraint. In all civilizations, and first and foremost, the garden represents space. Scale is all-important. Here therefore it must be limited, almost intimate, when it is a case of private dwellings, particularly in town — as indeed became abundantly clear with three little hidden gardens on the Herengracht that I had the opportunity of restoring.

Geometry

The great rivers which cross the country to flow into the North Sea have covered The Netherlands with marshes, lakes and rivers. These, from the moment when it was decided to drain such unproductive areas and make them fit for farming, were transformed by the multiplicity of drainage canals into the kingdom of the straight line, opening out complex geometries under an appearance of simplicity. This topography has always been represented in Dutch painting and gives it a powerful character. Everything is rectilinear. Whether it is a matter of watercourses, dykes, polders, roads and tracks, or even – as if by protective colouring – of gardens with their hedges, espaliered trees, paths grassed over or covered with seashells, all harmonize with the landscape. This mathematical, rigorous, peaceful and intellectual structure has always appealed to the Dutch, being both conducive to reflexion and suited to limited spaces.

Today, as in the seventeenth century, many Amsterdammers dream of owning a house beside the romantic River Vecht. Of the two hundred houses which stood along it in the Golden Age, more than half have disappeared, while others, such as the manor house of the interior decorator Gerry Meijer, have been restored.

Here a long pond accents the axis at right-angles to the house, which is surrounded by a long alley bordered on both sides by beds of roses and herbaceous plants, while the river banks are covered with thick turf. Pots of agapanthus decorate the terrace behind the house where the owner has indulged her taste for ornament. Here she has created a pattern of box hedges interspersed with lead vases and wooden benches. This superb garden designed by Dick Beyer is the

Dividing it into compartments compensates for the smallness of the garden of the War Institute on the Herengracht (top).

The banking establishment next door has had its garden remodelled in classical style. The eye is attracted by a statue glimpsed through an arbour of greenery (above).

Behind the Prince Bernhard Foundation there is a classical garden with parterres of box hedges and clipped shrubs (opposite).

perfect complement to the warm opulence of the decoration inside the house.

It was probably on the occasion of his embassy to the court of King George III in 1760–62 that Jacob Boreel succumbed to the charms of the English gardens designed by William Kent, Charles Bridgeman and Lancelot (Capability) Brown, and he sought to re-create their atmosphere in his Beeckestijn estate. He thus introduced into The Netherlands a fashion that was to dominate the whole of landscape gardening for over a hundred and fifty years, breaking with the original park design in the French style with its rectilinear or diagonal axes and its sense of rigid geometry based on hedges severely clipped as if to contain nature. Beeckestijn, apart from its very individual charm, is of great interest for its combination of different styles, apparently quite contradictory but each seeking in its own way to provide an answer to an enigma: nature.

While Boreel respected the classical nature of the gardens immediately surrounding the mansion, he created by contrast a very fluid arrangement for the park beyond, allowing it to maintain a natural relationship with the surrounding countryside. Apart from its importance in the history of style in landscape gardening, Beeckestijn deserves our attention for other reasons, not least because it contains one of the last surviving serpentine walls in The Netherlands. These brick walls, six to ten feet high and following a wavy course, had been devised as a protection against wind and frost. Indeed, the niches created by them could be used for growing fruit trees which could not otherwise have stood up to the weather. The heat stored up in the bricks during the day was enough to create micro-climates encouraging plant growth while at the same time offering the advantages of both open air and greenhouse.

The landscape style introduced at Beeckestijn was to have a widespread influence on the conception of gardens in the future. It has now been wonderfully restored, with a freedom of design that leaves plenty of scope for new ideas. The great herb-garden is bounded by the serpentine wall with its fruit trees. Further on, a pretty stone fountain standing in a pond and the flowerbeds with their rose arbours contribute to the total harmony, while in spring wild flowers carpet the lawn under the old trees.

All along the Vecht is a line of low houses built for the workers of a glass factory which no longer exists. These little houses have been restored, to become the privileged retreat of a number of architects and musicians. Thus Jan Willem ten Broeke, Director of the Centre for Netherlands Music, and his wife Henny have created a strictly modern garden in a very geometric style, its volumes and levels disposed with almost mathematical precision to give nature an abstract dimension which has great charm. Space is organized logically around two dense lawns. Here

The house of the talented interior decorator Gerry Meijer on the banks of the Vecht is reflected in an elegant pool at right angles to its façade (below left).

A traditional leisure activity of the occupants of the riverside properties along the Vecht is to watch the endless procession of passing boats. The creator of the park by the river belonging to Jan Willem and Henny ten Broeke designed it as a forestage to the show (above).

The severe lines of the herb garden in the park of Muiden Castle are seen here in springtime with the cherry trees in flower. In summer, the garden abounds in medicinal, tinctorial and aromatic plants on a grey-green ground dotted with many-coloured flowers (right).

and there, a piece of sculpture makes an unexpected appearance as a focal point for a perspective or as an anchor for spaces which would lack definition without it. A sculpture by the contemporary artist André Volten is the high point of the garden. It consists of a monumental brass cube whose large dimensions do not prevent it from integrating perfectly with the swaying shrubs and scented roses of its environment. Here the tangible and the intangible are placed in a new perspective and keep up a new dialogue.

The Passion for Flowers

Queen Juliana is an avid collector of lathyrus. Her passion has never wavered since she abdicated in 1980 in favour of her daughter. Each year she is bent on achieving the earliest, the most beautiful and the biggest flowers.

Gardening is one of the great passions that bind the Dutch nation together, a sort of second nature. It is no surprise to find that they have created so many varieties of that modest bulb, the tulip, their national flower. Carolus Clusius (Charles de L'Ecluse), who introduced the bulb into The Netherlands in 1592, would be amazed at such success if he could see it today. Curator of the Leiden botanical garden, he had already had a distinguished career as prefect under the Emperor Maximilian of Austria.

The botanical garden Hortus Bulborum at Limmen, north of Amsterdam, still possesses some specimens of the species cultivated by Clusius as well as the most important varieties later bred in the country, from the old-fashioned ones to new hybrids and late-flowering plants. Confronted by such profusion, the gardener should always remember the principle declared by the architect Mies van der Rohe: Less is more.

At the end of the 18th century there were more than two hundred country houses on the banks of the Vecht. There are still some spectacular examples remaining, such as Admiral Tromp's at 's-Graveland (below); or Rupelmonde (bottom), built at the end of the 18th century.

In the Limmen museum you can see the first wild tulips imported from Russia and the famous Constantinople tulip brought back in the 16th century by a naturalist from Leiden (opposite).

This living museum of bulbs displays, in particular, seventeenth- and eighteenth-century tulips, which are enjoying a new popularity among both amateurs and professionals anxious to preserve or restore old gardens. The national collection of bulbs is protected and lovingly tended. Apart from tulips, there are also new varieties of narcissus, fritillaries and hyacinths. There are often wild bulbs on show, brought back long ago from Asia Minor and Central Asia. This garden is a source of inspiration for the visitor, helping him to choose between an infinity of delicately differentiated modern varieties as well as among the historic bulbs available.

Rupelmonde is undoubtedly one of the most beautiful estates on the banks of the Vecht. Built in the late eighteenth century, the house seems to rise out of the water with its severe façade articulated by high windows and an elegant cornice. Each spring, to the delight of the owners and their guests, the immense lawn in front of the house is covered with a carpet of mauve and white. The branches of the ancient oak trees, still bare of leaves, rustle above a field thick with crocuses, which last several weeks and herald the coming of spring.

Professor van Rossum's estate at Leeuwenburg contains one of the Vecht's riverside tea-houses. Built in 1800 and newly repainted yellow under a thatched roof, it is the ideal viewpoint from which to enjoy the domesticated wild flowers which are the special feature of this garden, descendants of bulbs brought back from Asia Minor by Frisian horsemen. Since then they have multiplied, as they do naturally, with the lawn blossoming blue under the admiring eyes of people cruising by on the river: several varieties of crocus, including *tomasinianus*, and a host of

scillas cover the lawn under the age-old trees. Out of sight behind a yew hedge are two flower gardens, one of old roses, the other of white and yellow perennials, that are a joy to behold in summer.

William Henry Singer, an American painter and heir to the industrial empire which bears his name, was attracted by the atmosphere of the colony of artists who had settled at Laren since the beginning of the century. In 1911 he decided to move there to paint. The immense, luxurious house in which he was to die in 1943 was turned into a museum, opened by his widow in 1956, where not only his own paintings but works by Boudin, Corot, Van Dongen, Daubigny and Bonington are on show, together with statues by Bourdelle and Rodin and a goodly collection of antiques and old furniture from France, Italy, Germany and China.

Singer's special affection for rhododendrons has left its mark on the garden, where they flourish amidst magnificent trees. Each year there is a horticultural show there – Herfstflora, a celebration of autumnal flowers – which attracts people from all over this region that has been so blessed by the beauty of nature.

In springtime, the sturdy branches of the ancient oaks put out their first shoots above a solid mass of crocuses, which last for several weeks announcing the fine days to come.

One of the parks that have had great influence in Holland is the Thijsse Park at Amstelveen, named after a famous botanist who had created an earlier park at Bloemendaal, where he already gave a special place to wild flowers, putting into practice a rare branch of horticultural art. The Amstelveen park, designed by C.P. Broerse, extends over six hectares (fifteen acres), and was created specifically as a park for the villas of this new development south of the city. Beneath the trees, ferns, anemones, wild garlic (*Allium ursinum*) and hundreds of woodland and field flowers flourish. Although the peaty soil retains a humidity that makes it hard to find the right plants, there is an astonishing variety on show as a result of the efforts of J. Landwehr, assistant to C.P. Broerse and a great expert on peat-bog flora.

All year round the walker can find flowers to enjoy: spurges, gentians, heathers, wild bulbs. This park gave many amateur gardeners the idea of using wild flowers in the creation of their own gardens. Amstelveen has become, in this respect, a model for the wave of rediscovery of wild plants and flowers, showing how their delicacy can rival the beauty of cultivated species.

When a gardener decides to organize his garden round a single plant species, he runs the risk of monotony. While he is sure to achieve rigour and cohesion in this way, such a systematic approach could be tedious. The owner of a little house at Amstelveen has succeeded in avoiding just that hazard. Here ferns reign everywhere and they have all been selected from the fine-leaved varieties in order to spread a gossamer-like veil over the space between house and road. Against

The little thatched rustic tea-house adds to the charm of Professor van Rossum's huge garden. From early February to late April the great lawn, which stretches down to the Vecht, is carpeted with wild bulbs like the many-coloured crocuses (above). These follow the snowdrops and are succeeded in their turn by scillas and a multitude of other, pale-blue crocuses.

The American painter William Singer, heir to the world-famous family business, became obsessed in the early 1900s by Laren, an artists' colony. The splendid villa where he died in 1943 has been turned into a museum with a fine collection of paintings and sculpture. The pergola leading to the Greek pavilion is smothered with greenery in summer (opposite).

this swaying background, a pretty rococo bench in white-painted cast iron, standing against the house, is surmounted by an ornament with a floral motif made from the same material. A wide patch of *Hosta glauca* 'Robusta' with its blue-streaked leaves creates a transition between the bed of ferns and the contrasting white of the decorative ironwork. A *Hydrangea petiolaris* grows up the side of the house, its white clusters elegantly echoing the ornaments.

Ashlar paving-stones mark a winding foot-path through the middle of the ferns. Several evergreen varieties cluster round a *Skimmia*. This low bush has grown to a beautiful shape here, looking like a natural sculpture of variegated leaves and red berries.

During the war, the painter Maria Hofker and her husband were forced to live in Bali by the Japanese troops occupying what is now Indonesia. When they returned to Amsterdam at the end of the war they could only find a flat to live in. They then hit on the original idea of purchasing one of the innumerable workers' allotments on the outskirts of the city. Although their plot is a small one, they have arranged it with meticulous care, installing a little wooden cabin where they can have tea and keep their painting materials. A vine-shaded arbour serves as a studio on fine days. Perennials have multiplied and taken over the space, its small size forgotten beneath the spell of the garden's charm. The apothecaries' rose (*Rosa mundi*), angelica, countless geraniums, larkspur and erigerons give this dense, unpretentious garden an undeniably poetic atmosphere.

The famous botanist J.P. Thijsse, who dedicated himself to Dutch flora, gave his name to the wonderful garden at Amstelveen near Amsterdam, where wild plants can be seen growing in a beautifully planned natural habitat. On the peaty soil grow several varieties of ferns, as well as anemones and wild garlic (above).

In early spring, the pale-pink flowers of *Petasites hybridus* peep above its large round leaves (right).

Azaleas and the red horse-chestnut *Aesculus carnea* 'Briotii' add a vivid touch of colour to the Braak Park, which with the Thijsse Park makes a botanical ensemble unique of its kind. There the visitor can find wild plants and flowers as fine as any cultivated varieties (above).

One of the villas built on the edge of the Thijsse Park has a wonderful garden of ferns and climbing hydrangeas, *Hydrangea petiolaris* (left).

The Ever-present Water

In this country where nearly a quarter of the land is below sea-level, water is both a real menace – which a series of dyke-building projects is supposed to have averted for ever – and an object of great admiration. Its beauty has earned it a prominent place in the gardens of great mansions as well as in parks. Since the seventeenth century, fountains and ornamental ponds have adorned Dutch gardens, although they cannot be compared with cascades and fountains in the Italian style, given the lack both of space and of natural slopes.

From the classical garden to the garden of the present day, it is perhaps the use of water that has evolved more than any other feature: from the role of establishing boundaries in an architectural context – the digging of little narrow canals to delineate a boundary is a traditional Dutch practice – to the status of a kind of false but natural element at the end of the eighteenth century, until finally today it is looked on as a basic feature in shaping the framework of a planting scheme.

In Maria Hofker's tiny 'worker's garden', the massed flowers are pure poetry (left). There is a little arbour of vines which can also be used as a studio (right).
In this small paradise which Maria Hofker tends with infinite care, *Gillenia trifoliata* (Indian physic) confronts the climbing rose 'Paul Scarlet' (opposite).

214

The restaurant De Beukenhof, established in the twenties by Leonard van Putten in a building of lime-washed brick dating back to the fifteenth century, midway between Amsterdam and The Hague, was originally intended to entertain clients who visited his nursery garden in the village of Oegstgeest. From its beginnings as a simple tea-shop and nursery, this spot was very soon offering some of the finest food to be had in The Netherlands, to the point where the nursery has now been abandoned in favour of the famous restaurant whose garden is among its main attractions.

Leonard van Putten had studied the art of gardening under Sir Edwin Lutyens and Gertrude Jekyll during the early years of this century. Heir to a bulb merchant, he went into business with a friend who had studied architecture at Nijmegen.

The garden is clearly in the tradition of the English Edwardian style of architecture, with much use of pergolas smothered with wistaria, small buildings, and pools cunningly designed to look completely natural, and with clematis trained up wires to form a dome which thus becomes the focal design point of one of the gardens. The whole area is thickly planted with flowers and the richness of the colours inevitably recalls some of the loveliest English creations; but it is water that unifies the complex composition. The mere reflection in a little runnel, or the brilliance of an irregularly shaped stretch of water, is enough to impart a romantic touch. Here water brings a new facet to a profusion which never degenerates into confusion and which seventy years' loving care has preserved in a state of ideal perfection.

The restaurant De Beukenhof began in the twenties as a simple tea-room for customers of the nursery garden in the village of Oegstgeest, and gradually became a meeting-place for lovers of good food as well as gardens. The garden here is divided by rectilinear pools beside which rhododendrons and hydrangeas flourish (above).

At De Beukenhof, the frank artificiality of these reflecting pools is complemented by potted plants and the enigmatic carved heads which strike a dreamy note beneath the windows (right).

Queekhoven is one of the most charming properties on the banks of the Vecht. Situated at Breukelen – the village which gave its name to Brooklyn – the estate had a most turbulent history from its beginnings in the seventeenth century. It was devastated by Louis XIV's army before being completely rebuilt by an unknown architect, but its troubles did not end there.

The name of *zandpad* (sandy path) for the road that leads to the house goes back to the time when it was reached by a towpath. In the early years of this century, C.W. Matthes, a passionate orchid-lover, bought the property and laid out an 'English' garden there. It was planted with magnificent trees and shrubs, including maples, beeches, magnolias and rhododendrons.

The garden of Queekhoven is still among the largest along the Vecht and is still astonishing in its variety of trees, its meadows, and the old-fashioned air of its kitchen garden and flowers. You can still see the old greenhouse where a vine grows, fertilized each autumn with ox-blood that soaks into the soil, nourishing it and ensuring the high quality of the dessert grapes. Many such ancestral customs are still observed here.

The water that meanders through the park also runs beside an impressive avenue of yews – sixty of them, the same number as there are beads in a rosary.

It is not long ago that people still believed camellias would suffer from frost in The Netherlands. Not true. In some properly sheltered spots they grow very well. Some New Zealand varieties and species can even stand up to the winter.

One of the most spectacular collections of camellias planted in the open is at Haarlem, in a garden where an ancient beech tree had been cut down, allowing the sun's rays to penetrate and encouraging the growth of flowers and plants.

Another garden beside the Vecht, that of Queekhoven, is one of the most notable in this region for its outstanding collection of trees and shrubs: magnolia, sycamore, oak, beech and many varieties of rhododendrons and hydrangeas form a rich tapestry of greenery and well-planned colour from May to November. The 'pink bouquet beside the pond' is *Hydrangea macrophylla* (above).

Gunnera manicata spreads out its enormous bowl-shaped leaves by the edge of one of the pools in the Queekhoven garden. This giant plant native to Brazil acclimatizes very well to the damp soil of Dutch gardens. Its leaves are said to be the largest in the whole vegetable kingdom (opposite).

Where the tree stood, a small clearing catches the light and round it grows a multitude of different herbaceous plants as well as perennials whose pink, blue and violet colours give added emphasis to the space.

Camellias grow near the gable-end of the house on the north side. It is an ideal spot, and the original tiny shoots have already grown to a considerable height, thanks to the shade and heat provided by the house. Friends and plant-lovers are invited to visit as soon as the pink, crimson and white flowers come into bloom. So the reputation of this fine Asiatic shrub increases, whereas at first it was thought to be fit only for pots or the orangery.

Holland has always been known for its soil, which is so favourable to the cultivation of bulbs. Such soil needs to be sandy but not too poor, as it is along the North Sea coast behind the dunes. Bulbs have been grown since the sixteenth century at Limmen, Lisse, Hillegom and Sassenheim, making Amsterdam one of the hubs of the international trade and the Aalsmeer flower auctions, on the edge of the city, the world's largest flower market.

Jan Bader is one of the foremost traders in this field, and his company, Onderwater, is expanding rapidly. He exports bulbs to the United States, Canada and Great Britain. To receive his clients in an appropriate setting, he has acquired a huge house at Sassenheim where his wife has transformed the former meadows into a wonderful pleasure-garden. The first section consists of a large pond fringed with perennials leading to a garden in many shades of green, then to an orchard. The formal garden was the last to be laid out and planted with roses, herbaceous plants and perennials. Its luxuriant blossoms can be seen from the house. Bulbs are grown in the area round the pond. Apart from the mass and profusion of colours which give this garden its great charm, it is also a valuable centre for the study of new species.

In the garden of Tineke and Jan Bader, grape hyacinths make a lovely background to the daffodils (top). A circular brick path runs between a rose-bed and the flowering sage *Salvia superba* 'Ostfriesland' (above). Beyond the great pools and wide lawns there is a garden of roses and perennials (right).

A modern garden in Haarlem, behind an old house by a canal, is particularly remarkable for its collection of camellias (left).

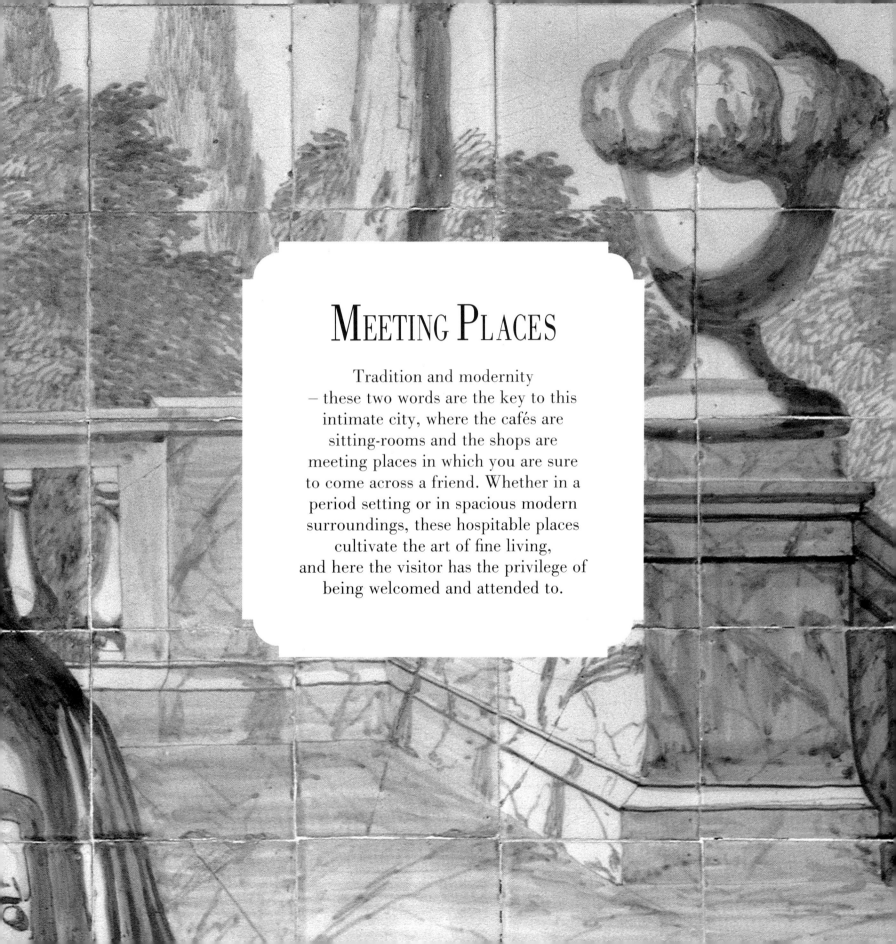

MEETING PLACES

Tradition and modernity
– these two words are the key to this
intimate city, where the cafés are
sitting-rooms and the shops are
meeting places in which you are sure
to come across a friend. Whether in a
period setting or in spacious modern
surroundings, these hospitable places
cultivate the art of fine living,
and here the visitor has the privilege of
being welcomed and attended to.

CAFÉS

The Dutch do not often invite people to their homes. They prefer to meet in friendly, convivial public areas which they use as an extension of their own sitting-room, such as the traditional *bruine kroegen* ('brown cafés') which have serenely watched fashions come and go over the years since the Golden Age. Walls yellowed by nicotine, small tables, old stoves, mellow panelling, gleaming beer pumps (3) and sometimes, as at **'t Papeneiland** (9), walls tiled in old Delft – this is the typical décor of the brown cafés where some of the brightest moments of social life take place. Not forgetting the indispensable reading-table (10, 12, 13) which no Dutchman worthy of the name could live without and which offers customers a wide selection of newspapers. It is not unusual for them to settle down in a café for hours at a time to read the papers, or to play chess or billiards or *klaverjassen*, a local version of bowls which is played, for example, in the backroom of **De Druif**, a brown café behind the docks (2, 4). The Dutch concern for a comfortable environment leads some firms to create rest-rooms for their employees – pleasant, sometimes unexpected places such as the unusual cafeteria for employees of the Stadsherstel, one of the biggest associations for restoring old houses, which has been set up in the old **Amstelkerk** church (8). One of Amsterdam's best-known brown cafés, the **Hoppe** (1, 3) is the favourite meeting place of journalists. Smoke-filled and noisy, with sawdust on the floor, its narrow room is nearly always packed and in summer often spills out on to the square. Just as the Dutch appear unaware of the use of curtains in windows, they waste no time, as soon as the fine weather comes, in moving their

11

12

13

lives outdoors on to the steps of their houses and the café terraces.

On one of the prettiest canals in the Jordaan, the picturesque old quarter much favoured by artists and craftsmen, **'t Smalle** (5, 14, 15, 16) has its own pontoon floating on the water. This charming *eetcafé* – literally, 'eating café'; they serve light meals – shows no sign of its great age. Behind its tall stained-glass windows there are a few tables where you can sit in peace to enjoy a lunch of *broodjes* (luscious filled sandwiches) with a salad. In these traditional settings, souvenirs of the great sailing-ships inevitably crop up to recall Amsterdam's past role as a busy port. Navigation lights and compasses seem to watch over the blood-red walls of the *eetcafé* **De Zeilvaart** (6, 7) at the far end of the harbour.

Since the eighties, Amsterdam has seen the arrival of cafés in a quite different style. In contrast to the warm, dark atmosphere of the brown cafés, their décor is strictly modern and they favour vast spaces inundated with light, as in the splendid **De Jaren** (10, 11), whose proprietors have done a remarkable job creating a perfect example of the modern trend with huge rooms and terraces looking directly out over the Amstel.

There are also some remarkable decorative schemes which have preserved the inimitable and flamboyant style of the early years of this century. With its geometric harmonies of marble and murals, the **Café Américain** (13) on the Leidseplein has barely changed since it was opened in 1902 and is still a most agreeable place at any time of day. As for the **Wildschut** (17) situated facing that masterpiece of the Amsterdam School, the Roelof Hartplein, it has a wonderful show-business atmosphere with theatre seats and decorations salvaged from a 1920s cinema.

14

15

16

17

1

2

3

STRONG DRINK

When the population of Leiden was decimated by plague in the seventeenth century, a young doctor who had learned from monks how to brew a concoction of various herbs to avert the contagion had the idea of distilling it to make it keep longer. Gin had been born. According to Kees van Wees (3) owner of one of the oldest distilleries in the country (5, 6), 'Good gin is made from several kinds of grain and distilled with juniper berries and different varieties of herbs' (7). Apart from gin (*jenever*), the range of traditional Dutch liqueurs is extremely wide. Some very sweet ones are made from fresh produce. More classic are the spirits distilled from fruits. Yet others, adorned with poetic names, keep up the tradition of the monk-physicians who invented them for specific uses, such as 'Rose without thorns', specially prepared to sweeten the breath of young girls. A syrupy liqueur, *Oranje Bitter*, is drunk all over the country on the Queen's birthday in honour of the House of Orange.

Whether in the centre of Amsterdam, where **De Drie Fleschjes** (2) flaunts superb decorations of the seventeenth century; or on a minor canal, like the **Hooghoudt** (4) installed in a vast warehouse of the same period; or in a neighbouring town like Haarlem, where **In den Uiver** (1, 8) occupies a former fishmonger's shop decorated with a splendid nineteenth-century mosaic mural – everywhere in The Netherlands gin has its temples, the *proeflokalen*. On their counters, in front of the rows of seasoned casks, you must observe a ritual which consists of leaning over a little glass, filled to the brim, to suck up the richly flavoured alcohol without picking up the glass and without losing a drop.

4

5

6

7

TRADITIONAL FLAVOURS

Travellers in past centuries were amazed by the huge appetites of the Dutch, whom they describe in their accounts as devouring copious quantities of plain country food. Dutch cooking has gained an undeserved reputation for heaviness, which dies hard. Some customs have not changed – the coffee break with delicious little butter biscuits is sacred – and the Dutch menu still contains such traditional dishes as pea soup, meat-and-vegetable stews, and the judicious use of exotic spices.

However, under the aegis of imaginative young chefs who, while looking to the old ways for inspiration, constantly invent new light and delicious recipes, traditional cooking has taken on a fresh lease of life. Their first rule is to use only local produce – young herrings available in May, smoked eel (5), seafood from Zeeland, endives, asparagus (which even has its own festival), Limburg fruit, etc.; Holland's soil is incomparably fertile.

The restaurants, like the cafés, display a contrast between the old decorative style of the Golden Age and the adventurousness of those who go for a modern style of decoration by the most fashionable contemporary designers. At the superb, traditional **D'Vijff Vlieghen** (4), its walls hung with Rembrandt etchings, at **De Blauwe Parade** (2) whose woodwork is surmounted by a wonderful frieze in late-nineteenth-century Delft tiles depicting a procession of singing and dancing children (see p. 1), or at **De Hoop op d'Swarte Walvis** (7) with its amazing fireplace in brown Delft tiles, the gourmet can enjoy traditional dishes and local produce in an old-fashioned setting; while at **Het Tuynhuys** (3), for example, the more limited

menu reflects the style of this fashionable spot with its huge, brightly coloured rooms and delightful garden, transformed by the photographer and designer Kees Hageman from a former *koetshuis* (coach-house). Lovers of the *années folles* of the turn of the century will find what they are looking for on platform 2B of the Centraal Station in the big café-restaurant **Eerste Klas** (1).

Thanks to the initiative of three friends who organize dinner-parties by special arrangement in their own homes, you can also dine and spend the evening in the private dining-room of a typical Amsterdam canal house: on the Keizersgracht with **Charlotte Bentinck** (6) or on the Herengracht at the home of **Patricia van den Wall**. **Kyra ten Cate** serves meals by candlelight in a fabulous eighteenth-century ship-chandlery (8).

In the Dutch gastronomic league, cheese takes first place. There is no greater pleasure than to find, during a country stroll, one of the cheese-farms which make *boerenkasen* – young farmhouse cheeses made from raw milk – in the traditional way. You can follow the different stages of this process in the picturesque village of Zaanse Schans with its green-painted wooden houses, at **Catharina Hoeve's** cheese manufactory (9), or in Broek in Waterland at the farm of **De Domme Dirk** (10). But mature Gouda, with a flavour as subtle as that of old Parmesan, is also well worth tasting and enjoying. Matured for three or even five years, as at this drying-house in Hoorn (11), these cheeses make a perfect accompaniment for an aperitif.

SPICE ROUTES

The great sailing vessels of the Golden Age used to return from distant voyages bringing all kinds of spices and other rare and costly products to stock the sumptuous markets of Amsterdam. Chocolate, tea and coffee became the favourite drinks of high society. To this day, at Christmas, the Queen pours out with her own hands the hot chocolate which she offers to members of her court and to her staff. In 1980 an Amsterdam woman called Jenny van Aken began to amass a collection of old chocolate boxes and cocoa tins (6) which now numbers 2,800 examples and is listed in the *Guinness Book of Records*. It tells the story in pictures of the chocolate factories which long ago moved away from the city centre. In Amsterdam, however, it is still possible to find some wonderful shops that offer exotic products in settings whose elegance remains unaffected by time. At **Hajenius** (1, 2) a rich, masculine aroma of Havana tobacco floats above the sumptuous turn-of-the-century décor. In Zaanse Schans, **Heijn** (5), a former grocer's shop converted into a museum, exhibits everything that a seafarer could possibly require, while Mr Heijn, who began by selling door-to-door, is today the head of a chain of supermarkets. At **Keijzer** (9) they still prepare the individual blends of tea and coffee which have delighted generations of clients; while at **Wijs & Zonen** (3, 4, 8) on the Warmoesstraat a changeless ceremony takes place every week when a taster comes to check the correctness of their own subtle blends of tea. Not far away, the chemist's and herbalist's **Jacob Hooy** (7), which has belonged to the Oldenboom family for two hundred years, is as successful as ever, thanks to its old-fashioned charm.

1

2

3

4

SWEET DREAMS

The different districts of Amsterdam are like so many villages, each with its own special charm. The **Ambassade** (4), which occupies eight seventeenth-century houses on the Herengracht, receives guests with attentive friendliness; only the quacking ducks disturb the early-morning stillness. On the Keizersgracht, visitors would do well to choose **Het Canal House** (1, 5), a plainer establishment decorated with furniture and objects selected with affection and imagination. On one of the town's oldest canals, a former town hall converted to a luxury hotel, **The Grand** (7, 8), may surprise visitors with its historic décor: its walls tell the story of six centuries of architecture, and one of the lounges (where marriage ceremonies used to take place, including that of Queen Beatrix) is absolutely spectacular with Art Nouveau murals and stained glass by Chris Lebeau. To enjoy the bucolic charm of the Vondelpark district with its big mansions of the early 1900s concealed in lush gardens, the most likely choice of hotel is the **Toro** (6), where the bedrooms look out over the lake; but if you prefer to open your windows to fresh sea breezes, you had better go on to Volendam, a picturesque port on the IJsselmeer, where at the **Spaander** (2, 3) the bridal suite has not changed since the seventeenth century and includes a small box bed built into the woodwork. In the hospitable bar (9), the walls are covered with pictures donated by the artists who were regular visitors. Back in Amsterdam, on the Amstel, a gracious welcome awaits in the splendidly decorated entrance hall of the **Amstel Hotel**, a magnificent nineteenth-century building whose recent closure for renovation prevented it from being illustrated here.

5

6

7

8

1

2

BEAUTY SALONS

When the Dutch go out, they feel the need to find a world which reproduces the intimacy of their jealously guarded homes, and this has led them to become past masters of the art of concealing every functional aspect of even the most everyday places. Some beauty salons are decorated in such a remarkable way that they deserve a visit simply for the pleasure of looking at them.

The establishment of the hairdresser **Michael** (1, 2) receives its clients in a former garage in which furniture designed by Berlage and De Bazel (collection of the proprietor) and engraved and stained-glass windows, one signed by the famous Theo Nieuwenhuis, make it look more like a sitting-room furnished with museum pieces. Other works by Nieuwenhuis can indeed be admired in the Rijksmuseum (see p. 239) or at the antique dealer Frans Leidelmeijer (see p. 250). The men's hairdresser **P.J. Janse** (3) has set up his salon in a former postoffice and decorated this authentic thirties setting with a unique collection of objects, furniture and accessories of the early 1900s. One window still has its original glass with an etched design showing a barber giving a head massage (5).

As for Bob Snabel, he provides a splendid contradiction to those who think of a sauna as merely a place where you go to lose half a pint of sweat. His **Sauna Déco** (4), furnished and decorated with all sorts of objects dating from around 1900 – glass, staircases, woodwork and light fittings which once adorned the Bon Marché in Paris – is a place of rare eclecticism where clients can read, play chess, chat or just enjoy the splendid surroundings.

3

4

ANTIQUES

In the Golden Age, ships were chartered by wealthy merchants to bring back whole cargoes of precious objects. Since these were so costly, the Dutch lost no time in copying them, and skilful and inventive craftsmen quickly discovered their own style, producing work of the highest quality. Thus in the seventeenth century potteries were founded at Delft to imitate the precious blue-and-white porcelain from China (4, Salomon Stodel collection). Master craftsmen of genius soon developed a special and unique kind of Delftware (5). One of the finest examples of this true ceramic art is the vast tile-picture in the Rijksmuseum which depicts a scene of wealthy burghers feasting on the terrace of a country house (see pp. 222–3). The house bears the date 1707, so presumably the work was made at that time. The famous factory De Porceleyne Fles (The Porcelain Bottle), founded in 1653, is the only one still in production today. It was the first to make the famous white Delft, of which Peter Gabriëlse owns some fine examples (6) and which, once confined to the kitchen, is now greatly sought-after. True porcelain was rare in The Netherlands. Some was produced at Weesp (1), Loosdrecht, The Hague and Amstel towards the end of the eighteenth century, but these factories were never as important as the fifty or so famous Delft potteries, an example of whose rare polychrome tiles dating from the seventeenth century is reproduced on pp. 4–5. Dutch craftsmen shone in every department. In glassware they had a reputation as engravers, and unique pieces were sent from all over the world to be decorated (see p. 88). They were also past masters in the art of decorative windows, stained or engraved (3, Weesp Town Hall). Cordovan

238

8

9

leather was imitated in the seventeenth century in Amsterdam's workshops (see p. 240, Inez Stodel collection), while also in the seventeenth century, Johannes Lutma, the greatest goldsmith of Amsterdam, developed the auricular style, whose complex volutes were later imitated by cabinet-makers (12, Dutch marquetry commode, Salomon Stodel collection). After his time, Dutch goldsmiths continued to produce masterpieces (2, silver kettle stamped DVG, 1774, Salomon Stodel collection) and more recently some beautiful silver-plated pieces (13, Boutique Silverplate).

In 1903, the architect H.P. Berlage revolutionized the aesthetic norms of his time. It is less well known that this inspired creative artist also designed furniture (9, desk, Vakbonds Museum). Reacting against his rational forms, the members of the Amsterdam School launched a more sensuous style (11, oak cupboard inlaid with ivory, signed Sluyterman, Frans Leidelmeijer collection). One of them, C.J. Blaauw, has left some furniture characterized by its association of curved forms with geometric structure (10, armchair, Frans Leidelmeijer collection).

The Rijksmuseum is a treasure-house of Dutch cabinet-making of all periods, such as the Art Nouveau sitting-room (8) created in 1909 by the famous Amsterdam designer Theo Nieuwenhuis (1866–1951), who was inspired particularly by Oriental art. Nowadays, the most unexpected examples of popular art become museum pieces, like the extraordinary barrel-organs signed Perlee (7). One of these, auctioned at Sotheby's, reached an astronomical sum worthy of the very finest furniture.

10

11

12

13